THE BRIDPORT

POETRY, SHORT STORIES A

JUDGES
Liz Berry • Poetry
Wendy Erskine • Short Stories
Jasmine Sawers • Flash Fiction

redcliffe

First published in 2024 by Redcliffe Press Ltd
e: info@redcliffepress.co.uk
www.redcliffepress.co.uk

Follow us on X @RedcliffePress
© the contributors

Follow The Bridport Prize:
Follow us on X and Instagram @BridportPrize

www.bridportprize.org.uk
www.facebook.com/bridportprize

ISBN 978-1-915670-20-5

Typeset in 10.5pt Times

Typeset by Addison Print Ltd, Northampton
Printed by Hobbs the Printers Ltd, Totton

Contents

We applaud your every word

Writing can be a solitary experience but within these pages you will discover community: people who want to, have to, need to tell a story. The words may flow in different forms yet each individual voice is loud and clear for all of us to hear.

In these divisive times, writing can bring joy, a distraction from the everyday. We are taken to places, meet characters and step into events carved from pure imagination. On dark nights, at the beach, on the bus, we become part of the page. Words matter. They are one of the greatest gifts human beings bestow on each other.

Thank you to everyone who believed in their words and trusted us to hold them tight for a while. They live long in our memory and within the pages of this anthology.

To all the writers who stumble around whether they are good enough, know that at one time or another, those within these pages thought exactly the same.

Be brave and believe people want to read what you have to say. Because we do.

Congratulations to all the writers honoured here. You are our pride and joy.

Keep writing.

The Bridport Prize Team

Where are they now?

Alyson Kissner
Alyson's winning Bridport Prize poem *Prayer w/o Punctuation* has gone on to be highly commended in the prestigious Forward Prize For Poetry's best single poem.

Amy Stewart
A Short Story Bridport Prize winner, Amy's debut novel *Hex House* will be published by Titan Books in 2026.

Allison Field Bell
Carve, Allison's winning Flash Fiction story was selected for inclusion in the Best Small Fictions anthology.

Sean Lusk
Sean's a former Bridport Prize Short Story winner who has now published his second novel *A Woman of Opinion* with Penguin Random House. It was also chosen as a Sunday Times historical fiction Book of the Month.

Lara Haworth
Monumenta began as a winning Bridport Prize short story and has since become an acclaimed debut novel published by Canongate.

LIZ BERRY

Poetry Report

Writing poems, when the world feels full of darkness, is a beautiful and reviving act. Poetry is a way of reaching out, of seeking understanding and shared humanity, of finding light or summoning the courage to gaze into the dark. To know that so many of you were writing poems and sending them out into the world this spring fills me with hope. I want every poet who entered the Bridport Prize this year to know that I read your poems with tenderness; your work and brave spirits lit up my summer days.

The best thing about judging a competition is discovering thrilling, fresh, moving poems, the kind of poems which make you want to send them to everyone you know and say: look at this wonderful thing! This year's submission pile was full of poems like this. What a joy!

The worst thing about judging is having to choose winners, as in many ways it feels counter to all that I love about poetry – the community and connection, the sharing and encouraging of creativity. I always get down to about twenty poems and want to stop as they're all fantastic. So I try to think of it not as "which is best?" but rather which poems would I most like to share with you and shine a light on now.

So, here they are: beautiful and brilliant in the full beam of the winning glow. I hope you'll enjoy them as I did and find something that touches or delights you.

Highly Commended:

Curlew
This poem is a musical, linguistic delight. Chock-full of gorgeous language, it brings the curlew to us in fresh and unexpected ways.

March Hare
An elegant poem with a pleasing jumpy form, echoing the jaggy energy of the hare, this piece conjures the artist Van Gough in his final months. The images are vivid and the desperation of the painter's illness makes for a heartbreaking end.

The Crack in the Road has Spoken

I'm always drawn to strange poems and this one has strangeness to spare. I couldn't stop thinking about it: its dark folkloric imagery, what it meant, whose voice we were hearing...

That glass of milk as a Western standoff

Whip smart and swift, this poem brilliantly and cleverly explores a moment of domestic struggle as parent and child face off over a glass of milk. The ending is so powerful. It's rare to find a poem that handles the subject of disordered eating with such sharpness and skill.

Rabbit

I so enjoyed this poem: lush and jittery, capturing all the wild energy of the sister who moves beyond the borders of the domestic world.

Pantoum for the Gujarati Aunties of North West London

How wonderful to discover a pantoum in the pile! I really enjoyed the vivid world this poem conjured – the colour and dance – and the way it moved seamlessly to the ordinary grit of life. Lovely stuff.

Passerine

This felt like a young woman's poem and I loved its visceral voice and the complicated chaos of the age it explores. It reminded me of Kim Addonizio's early poems. The mother in me wanted to reach into this poem and hold its speaker tightly!

The Old Country is Dying

There was something of the folksong about this curious, elegiac poem. I liked its easy, almost conversational, voice and the lush moments of lift offered by its nature imagery.

How to survive a road traffic accident

All the messy bravery and disappointment of being young are here, along with the smart rueful voice of experience. That last stanza is just brilliant!

Earth Day

Ah I was glad of this poem of gentle wonder and questioning. In a time which feels so overwhelming it's good to be reminded of the beauty of the world and its need for our awe.

Third:

Hope in Three Syllables
This was just the poem I needed in the complicated, heavy, summer days
when it found me. Plain-speaking and moving, it's a reminder of the
bravery we show when we allow ourselves to hope. I can imagine readers
sharing this poem with those they love and taking comfort from it on
dark days.

Second:

Ode to Io (Galileo's Song)
A beautifully crafted, powerful poem which brings together myth,
astronomy, history and love. From its bold opening address, it sustains a
dark, forceful energy as we move towards the "next hurtling place" of
loss.

First:

Other Words for Dancefloor
I adored this fizzy, clever, whirling list poem which conjures all the
energy, thrill and heartache of the dancefloor. An elegy for a student
nightclub (joy!) but also an elegy for youth, this poem is a delight to read
and I know many readers will connect with it too. Its panicky, urgent
ending conjures perfectly the ecstasy and grief of being young.

WENDY ERSKINE

Short Story Report

I don't know if you have ever shopped in TK Maxx (or, for those in the US, TJ Maxx). It's the type of store where it's absolutely pointless to have in mind something specific – a black coat, say. More sensible is to go with no particular expectation and rather, a receptiveness to whatever prospect might present itself as worthy of attention, be it a jumbo box of Korean sheet-masks, an angle-poise lamp, a velour tracksuit or kitchen knives. If this analogy does not seem facetious, I feel similarly about the Bridport Prize and short story competitions in general. I could blithely tell you what I am looking for: emotional truth, complexity of experience; tautness; innovation in form; the weight of the unspoken; fully realised worlds and so on. But in reality I have no idea what I'm looking for until it presents itself.

When reading, I tried to take each story on its own terms, approaching it with the flimsiest of expectations about what a story is and what it should do. Speculative fiction, the quotidian, the bizarre, the experimental, the traditional, the pained, celebratory, baffling, capricious, political, apocalyptic: there was no hierarchy of significance. I liked being surprised. Yet I also enjoyed writers bringing their own sensibility to familiar contexts.

In terms of the winners and highly commended stories, it's important to remember that personal preference should not masquerade as objective fact. I cannot say with conviction that these stories are the 'best.' That would be delusional. It just so happens that I like them. Another judge at another time might have made a different selection from the same stories. Hell, at another time, so might I. And perhaps I should also say, that although someone like Blindboy might, with extraordinary generosity, have described me as 'the greatest living short story writer', I have never myself ever won a competition of this kind. I'm aware too that some short stories acquire their power form being part of the gestalt of a collection, rather than being knockout standalone texts. Ultimately, so much is a question of taste and in this case, it's mine. But, all of that said, I feel so very proud of the highly commended and winning stories.

'Blue' tells a story of responsibility and projected escape. It's sharp, condensed and so alert to detail.

The story **'EDC'**, short for Every Day Carry, features Mitchell, who enjoys videos detailing the essential items that people have routinely on their person. It's a beautiful paean to the world of stuff and the talismanic qualities items can hold. And yet it's also about being a partner and being a parent.

'Grace', unshowy, unsentimental and ostensibly about a dog being put down, offers an unflinching portrait of a marriage. There is a hardness to this story, a steely stoicism, that I adored.

In **'Honey'**, an 'idiot woman' brings honey cakes to a man who sits on a small hill. Skilful in its alternating perspectives and its concrete, vivid language, it has the power and timelessness of myth.

'That Summer' controls effectively a large and disparate group of characters as it delineates so movingly the multiplicities of loss over a particular summer.

'The Butterfly Boy', written so cleanly and precisely, documents teen girlhood, swimming pools, rivalries with enviable clarity and intensity.

'The Second Coming' about Jesus returning to take his position in a high street made me laugh more than any other story. Who would've thought Jesus had an AC/DC tattoo? And yet this story is serious in what it has to say about consumerism, protest and injustices.

'They Cling Tightly' moves deftly and assuredly across different temporal lines as it tells a moving story about two brothers. Ideas of connection, responsibility and letting go receive delicate, careful treatment.

A daring, technically demanding story, **'Thump Thump'** is narrated by someone in an enclosed space, sipping a negroni. It's compelling and very skilful.

It's brilliant to come across a story with great dialogue and that's what I found in **'Western'** between the narrator, her mother and her boyfriend. Complexities of identity, tradition and place are explored in an illuminating, engaging manner.

And so in third place is **'The Offer'** about a trip to a firm that offers payment for those who want to forego treatment for terminal illness. It manages to do so many things: there's a deeply convincing set-up; a cool satire of bureaucracy and a compelling consideration of how much – or little – life amounts to.

'After The Fall' is a pitch-perfect, beautifully controlled story about the relationship between an ageing, married couple. But its's also about how and why we construct narratives. The ending of this story is superb in terms of its balance. It is a very deserving runner-up.

And finally, in first place, **'Zanzibar Blue'**. This is a story of remarkable lucidity and poise. The narrator, involved in academic study, stays in a guesthouse run by an Afrikaner, Papa, who intends to build a hotel called Zanzibar Blue. Exploitation, violence, the status of the outsider: our narrator observes it all with compelling nuance.

Judging the Bridport Short Story Prize was a privilege and actually surprisingly moving. There was something to admire in every single story. Thank you.

JASMINE SAWERS

Flash Fiction Report

What an honor to be asked to judge one of the finest flash contests in contemporary literature. The Bridport Prize attracts some of the most skillful writers working today, and they certainly did not make choosing between them easy. I am always blown away by the ingenuity and diversity of flash; while there is always room for traditional structures, the compressed form demands both writer and reader conceptualize narrative in new and exciting ways to deliver the punch to the gut found in the best fiction. For me, a surefire way to achieve potency within concision is to make the most of a story's unique voice.

Each of the highly commended stories spoke to me in a clear voice that gripped my emotions without devolving into sentimentality. In **'Flat Five'**, the second person narrator is so assured and confident while being acted upon by an outside force that will be their downfall. In **'The story we will one day never tire of telling you'**, the first person direct address narration explores the thwarted longing for a child alongside the sureality of blind parental love. In **'My Aunt Keeps a Spider in Her Hairnet'**, the first person narrator is not our protagonist but a witness to her actions, heightening the loneliness that pervades the prose. In **'Chicken'**, the second person narration is deployed expertly to enact alienation born from trauma. In **'Jenny's Mum Tells Lies'**, the child narrator delivers nuance beyond her ken amid the frustration of being at the mercy of self-absorbed adults.

The visceral evocation of pain, betrayal, and self-obliteration sets **'Love Bite'** apart from other stories of infidelity. The speculative bent serves a unique emotional realism: our protagonist would do anything to keep her husband's affections, but in doing so, destroys herself. Love, in this story, is consumption, is annihilation, is disappearance.

With its unique form, **'Eulogy of Henry Rowley, 1961-2024 (Notes)'** layers the oft-tread story of the death of a partner with gentle humor, a touch of resentment, and the quiet tragedy of getting older without one's beloved. The protagonist, self-deprecating and flinching from his own devastation, preoccupied with making sure others are kept comfortable in the face of his grief, shines even from his place in Henry's shadow.

On my first pass through the stories, I read them by order of submission date, oldest to newest. This meant that I read **'Enough'** last. When you read something last, there is a great deal stacked against it: your eyes and your mind are fatigued, the excellent pieces you read prior are crowding your brain and competing for your attention, the piece is quite literally being compared to more stories than any of the others. And yet when I read 'Enough', I knew immediately that it was the winner. It is a masterclass in expressing the unspeakable, in employing voice to shield and deflect, in exposing exactly the vulnerability the protagonist is trying so desperately to deny. The real story slithers between the lines, a creeping dread whose truth breaks over the reader with a chill even though the damning words are never uttered. In under 200 words, 'Enough' evokes fear, anxiety, hatred, and panic while exercising great restraint and never sacrificing the fineness of the writing. Even the absence of a full stop at the end carries meaningful narrative weight. If Ishiguro wrote flash, I believe it would look something like this.

Each of these stories defies expectation and imparts a heartache that lingers, all the heavier for their brevity. The best flash is honed into a bullet: it's in and out before you realize you've been hurt.

POETRY FIRST PRIZE

ROSALIND EASTON

Other Words for *Dancefloor*

i.m. Club Rococo, Exeter, 1996-2016

Device for measuring the tensile strength
of undergraduate friendships alchemised
in the distillery of freshers' week. The last will and testament
of someone's sixth-form romance. The blank page
of the essay you were supposed to be writing that evening.
Percussive instrument (treble: kitten and stiletto heels;
mid-range: Sambas and Gazelles; bass: eight-eye Docs
in black and cherry red). Crucible filled with Goldschlager,
Moscow Mule, vodka Red Bull, Marlboro Light ash,
sweat, tears, occasionally blood, cupped in the small hands
of Kylie and heated with a campus newsagent cigarette lighter.
For one glorious term only, an ornamental lake
on which the four of you glided like swans. After
the Easter break, a Scalextric track
for rumours, secrets and flat-out lies. The collision point
of two tectonic plates: BEST FRIEND and BOYFRIEND.
A plate glass window through which
tomorrow was thrown. Your heart as a letter, unfolded,
spread flat and glitterball-lit. A safety net made only of holes.
A trap door. A sinkhole. By June, an ice rink where
the three of them skated while you were
trapped underneath. And always, from the start, the panic-stricken face
of a clock, counting down your three years at hyperspeed,
seconds and minutes and hours pouring
down its cheeks and into the cracks,
gathering you all in its spindly arms,
ushering you to the exit before the whole thing
collapsed.

MELISSA KNOX EVANS

Ode to Io (Galileo's Song)

O priestess: sister: you — you, mortal
moon, orbital as an electron swinging
out from Jupiter's pull. Daughter of
Inachus, I need your divine, sulphuric
burn. Your ellipsis of tides. Need to
capture you as Zeus did — becoming
cloud and lowering myself over your
wildest form. This night as I find you,
my sister is busying her hands as usual,
sewing a shirt as I line up my glass
with Jupiter's wide mass. The doctors
say angina builds in her muscle and
vein and I feel this hard truth, the fade
in her eye. Everything, everything fades
but you, yellow as seduction: vast body,
fire, vast ice. You who have been horned,
a heifer, disguised from Hera's wrath,
then gifted and guarded under a giant's
hundred eyes. You who have been lost,
been wanderer, wet heat and gadflies
driving you unwilling and mad to the
Nile where Zeus knew you again —
touching you back into mortality
and childbirth, into motherhood of
gods. But this single, rippling night, I
know you like no other: your violence
of creation, blistering floodplains of
rough, liquid rock – tidally locked as are
our own revolutions – all of our bodies
eternally flinging themselves outward
to the ends of space. Even after we lose
faith. Even after the night my sister
wanes fully — passing on to her next
hurtling place.

CHRISSY BANKS

Hope in Three Syllables

All shall be well and all shall be well.
All manner of things shall be well.
> Julian of Norwich

Hope springs eternal, my mother would say.
She'd sigh a little, steel herself against self-doubt.

Tonight, a lemon moon's thin rind curves
against the dark. Its light will shine again, full-face.

When we lived in sad times, a pink rose grew impossibly
between concrete path and our house's outer wall.

Our dog's tail is electric. Eyes fixed on my face, this
labrador pants hope in three syllables: *Walk. Eat. Love.*

So many acts of hope: marry more than once; chant
a prayer; select a candidate and draw your X in the box.

When singers on their balconies in Rome launch
their high notes, something inside me also rises up.

A climber slips, falls into night, ice-crusted rock.
Inch by inch, he crawls the long trail home.

My mother would say, *All comes to she who waits.*
Perhaps – yet sometimes you must gather a search party.

Days of war, of plague and parting, her voice
breaks free from the ashes: *Where there's life, my love ...*

On a dark shore, a man waits for his ship to come in.
Or a dinghy. Whatever arrives, he will climb aboard.

FRANCESCA DUFFIELD

March Hare

In Dr Gachet's quiet house,
        this place of doors opening,   and closing,
        these March days
                are the cruellest, while colour leaps from the veins
of the almond trees,

                and this year's unreachable summer
        taunts with thin ribbons
                of trembling sun:
hard-fingered winter
crouches still, in the shadow
        where you sit unmoving
                by the high small window

but your never-resting mind
                is a mirror, a radiant
                        brief dazzle of illumination
and then in the dark cold hours,
        deep night,
                not sleeping,
                waiting

                for the whims of daylight, hungry
                        to savour the colours again

but they are never the same
        as the ones that vibrated,
                singing fiercely, yesterday   when the fire of them
        ran sharp

through   your blood   like a wonderful poison

March Hare

if that is madness,
        then you must be
                the March Hare,
                        shape-shifting,
        fevered by a force
                you cannot understand,

running wildly   in circles,
                        leaping, spiralling
           boxing with shadows,

shadow-circled
        eyes of light
           reflecting the moon,

                    silently weeping

ROSHNI GOYATE

Pantoum for the Gujarati Aunties of North West London

When autumn, with her damp air, nestles into the night,
the Gujarati aunties of North West London dress up.
In October, they descend upon school halls with their garba
tran tali, two steps forward, one step back.

The Gujarati aunties of North West London, all dressed up
are shapeshifters, time travellers, memory-keepers;
three claps, two steps forward, one step back,
they form spirals and dance, divine altar at the centre.

Shapeshifters, time travellers, faithful memory-keepers,
they are hairnetted assembly-line workers by day;
by night, they form spirals, dance around the divine altar,
jewels and sequins, bandhani and bangles, spinning.

Assembly-line workers by day, they remove their hairnets,
they trade in their blue overalls and plain saris for the night.
Adorned in jewels, spinning sequins, bandhani and bangles,
for nine nights and ten days they dance and pray.

Their blue overalls and plain saris are swapped out,
goddess Durga takes centre stage for the spectacle;
nine nights and ten days they dance and pray
to goddess of loyalty, mother of wisdom and knowledge.

Durga's reincarnate forms are the centre of the spectacle;
goddess of forgiveness, goddess of peace,
goddess of loyalty, mother of wisdom and knowledge.
Gujarati aunties are women of ritual, women of repetition,

dancing for the goddess of forgiveness, goddess of peace,
they offer flower petals like water, one pound coins.
I learn from these aunties, women of ritual, women of repetition,
protectors of their sons and daughters from the streets,

with offerings of flowers, one pound coins.
In the morning they'll return to their factory shift, clock in, clock out,
praying for protection for their children on the forgotten streets
of Neasden, Harlesden, Wembley, Kingsbury.

They return to their factory shifts, clock in, clock out,
underpaid shift workers, dodging muggers on their walks home
through Neasden, Harlesden, Wembley, Kingsbury.
Their kids settled into another year at underfunded schools,

underpaid shift workers, dodge muggers on their walks home.
In October they descend upon school halls for garba,
their kids settled into the year at underfunded schools,
as the damp autumn air, nestles into the night.

LUISA A. IGLORIA

Earth Day

My grandson listens to a science podcast
where children call in questions, all

prefaced by "But why"— But why is snow
white and sparkly? But why do people have

two eyes and yet see only one image? Why
do we call some species invasive, meaning

they're not indigenous to that environment?
Why and how did they move to where they

shouldn't be in the first place? Why should we
kill the spotted lanternfly, the brown stink bug,

nutria in marsh waters? Everyone is writing
about this world that is ending and ending,

or choking and soon on the brink. But it's still
a world in which I've not yet had the chance

to put my arms around the largest tree, not yet
stood hip-deep in water to applaud the homing

instincts of fish swimming against the current,
or welcome the pelicans back after their long

absence. Should we turn off the lights tonight
for an hour, and go outside to look at the stars?

Perhaps we should tell stories of what it was like
the first time we saw the moon rise into the dark

Earth Day

tablecloth of sky, gleaming silver platter free of
the need to serve bread or potatoes or stew. We

should hold the ticking minutes—pearls shaped
like small O's of wonder, which is what they are.

JOANNE KEY

The Crack in the Road has Spoken

when i am gone   who will be left
   to listen
hear you   silently weeping
   for the great tarmac king
         who lies sleeping so peacefully
in the land   of the dead
   these ten years past
         haven't we   danced a merry dance
around all this
   learnt to tread   carefully
         when we first found you
   out there   split   open
or patched up again
   black sticking plasters
               on all your cracks   and fractures
      as soon as one wound closes   another opens up
      and fills   with water
so no one really knows   how deep they go

the times i have to lie   awake and listen
   to things that have been left   open
the stifled cries   under my window
   my mind   on fire
      with the sounds of mouths   that don't know when to close
riddled   with the tinnitus whistling
of something   unhinged
   half forgotten songs   of wanderers
   on their long   and winding roads
christ   please just leave it alone
   i rue these wild   and treacherous nights
you dream him up
         out of that donkey jacket blackness
               see him taking shape   in the sticky tar pit
      of your smile   your eyes taped off

warning signs   glowing all around that single inky drop
of him
    dark ovum crowned in starlight
the sulphurous smell   of this bitumen alchemy
       as he pours out
          of the refinery   of the night
smooth and slick
          one part   man
      three parts   black ice

CLARE LABRADOR

Passerine

I'm a mountain shrike, I say, to impress
            a group of boys with pretty hands, heavy voices,
    tequila shots for everyone. By that I mean, I devour
by wailing or singing, chasing the sun and the sound of a heartbeat,
            by impaling, dissecting, and my bloodied mouth
                swallowing pieces and pieces of a soft animal.
 Down the corridor, a girl
wearing a sundress in the middle of December
takes off her shoes and walks herself home. I want her,
        I want to be her.
 But you're more like a swan, he tells me.
I read somewhere that swans drown themselves
when they lose their partner. Imagine being born
        into that type of predestined sorrow.
You don't know how to be alone, is what he wants to say.
I tell him my solitude wears many faces. Sometimes,
            she's throwing up when it's three am, in the bathroom, all over
            my bedroom floor, my dirty laundry, my tampered pills.
Sometimes, she's perched in the backseat of a stranger's car,
as she tethers herself to her body. Her mouth softened with alcohol,
        until the warning lights eat at her brain –
                tell the boy, *Let me out of the damn car*
What would it take to be as harmless as a hummingbird?
        To no longer ask for some kind
    of forgiveness, or redemption, or the promise of an end
    to this hunger for skin in the pit of my featherbed chest?
Is there anything tougher than a drunk twenty-year-old girl
    alone in a parking lot? I can't take off my shoes,
    but I am stumbling on the pavement, learning
how to walk with talons on my feet

SHANNA McGOLDRICK

The Old Country is Dying

It's just a lane;
could've been any lane,
but it was our lane.
Warped trees, wild hedgerows
lawless with stickyweed
and crawling with summer bees.
Look – singed light
runs off the barn roofs,
and round the bend –

It's just a house;
could've been any house,
but it was her house.
Still is. Look – touch these quiet walls,
windows kissed by the flare of the fields
whose long grasses brandish their embers at the sky.
This door handle, worn smooth by her homecomings.

What is a country anyway?
The old countries are dying
the way they always do.
Bleeding out
so softly that you mightn't notice.

This one is slow to leave. Look –
the fat sun hoses down the church, sticking to the lichen.
The cattle are heading home
down clear roads punctured with speed signs
and all the potholes patched.
Still, at the end of the day,
the grasses whisper in their fields.

What is a mother anyway?
Just someone you love madly,
over a life and down a lane.
And how many of them
have been scratched onto this land.
And how many quiet houses.

Still, look –
at the end of the day,
it was just a country.
(Could've been any country.)
Just a lane.

TOM McLAUGHLIN

Curlew

Come at daybreak, come at twilight,
come when the sea has receded,
the colour of the world on the turn,

your two-note cry as tense
as the reeds in the ebb current,
not a complaint but a riddle

solved by the swelling river;
crocheted mudlark at home
in residual stink; spindle-

shanks skirting the brim with dogged scrutiny;
knickerbockered whaup;
long-beaked goblin traipsing

the roof space at night; stilted nomad
tripping the blood-rich
sediment; ore-boned rainbird,

your scrape a sleek secret tucked
in dicey moorland grasses;
curlew as yardstick; curlew as guess;

curlew as vanishing endpoint;
weepy mendicant; vagabond godwit;
snug and ungainly panhandler

of the day's crevices, mudded
in ooze, whetting the estuary's silence,
soil-nested grubs pinioned by the light

of the hookbill's arc
curved in sympathy
with the sea's worried meniscus;

barely there, you merge
with the furze, drizzle-light
on the mudflats' mirror.

CHARLOTTE SALKIND

How to survive a road traffic accident

The one thing I'd promised my mother
was that I'd never get on a motorbike.
He met me at Madrid-Barajas with a second helmet

and I took it. I would have lived underneath his bed
if he had let me. The whole way back I thought about her face
when I was found impaled on the tarmac,

how we always made fun of her for worrying,
how she'd ask what we were doing and we'd send back gifs
of two women bungee-jumping in between a lion's jaws,

how the cancer grew quiet in her mother in the seventies,
how she walked in and saw her breast was missing.
My suitcase thudded into my back, I had so much love

and nowhere to put it. That night we had dinner
with his gorgeous Spanish girlfriend, who did pole on weekends
for fun and body confidence. I threw up behind a red sequoia

and continued living. I've got good at it. I drink water,
I wear my longing on its own six-centimetre string,
I barely notice where the metal meets the bone.

AMY WARD

Rabbit

The way she sat down was as if a rabbit
had been brought into the room,
already half out
bounding for a way back to the field.
The long muscles of her thighs
flexing their fast heat. Eyes in their burrowed
blue and early mist, nearly blind. Only the tree
or the wind itself could have kept her
in her seat – the knotted wood
of table legs rising past her knee
not enough to say that the shattering land
was here, somewhere, wild, guiding
either into the copse or on
to a distant outcrop. How easy it was
to lie in the middle of the world as if
in the lap of a parent and trusting them,
completely. But here, she could not
sit still – from sink to oven
and back again while I filled our mugs,
half of her eye, all of the time, split
like a thought, through the window. Her tall ear
not hearing the house shift in its footings – its own
root sucking back the land.
                                        Once before
when we were children, she said we close
ourselves in boxes, stack along roadways
like great unnamed objects in the cellar
of a dead archaeologist. I jumped after her
across the heath for many hours, teeth into
the ground of yellow grasses, light red
in her grey paws, until we were older –
until we heard the arguments of men
and picked our sides. And while I kept thinking,
as a person does of their big sister, that she

had been right somehow, anciently, she tunnelled
too deeply into the warrens, welts rising
darkly between her claws. Whenever she came by,
regardless that the rooms were mine, regardless
of their growing, she visited half-startled,
always in a loose moment of running.

CATHERINE WILSON GARRY

That glass of milk as a Western standoff

A shot of my eyes narrowing,
then yours. This table isn't big

enough for both of us and my unspoken
problem. The one that hangs its hat on

every dinner time or cracks a lasso
like a noose. We've run this game

before, and all the others too –
bent over the same table

like we're betting our lives on
cards. There's one where

you reheat the same plate for
each meal, just like your own

father did. The one where you
bargain and beg before you lock

the bedroom door that doesn't
fully cover up the sounds

you make, the ones like an animal
that is being beaten. Tonight,

we'll sit until I drink this milk,
the cold night already pooling

on the concrete floor. The audience
thinks I'm stubborn, like a wild horse

That glass of milk as a Western standoff

that needs to be broken. If they just
looked closer at that horse, they'd see how

its spit froths over, how it widens its
eyes so it can take in everything. How

all you can see is the white.

JOE BEDFORD

Zanzibar Blue

Papa's guesthouse was situated among a grove of coconut trees at the western edge of the village. Mine was the smallest room of six but it had a bed and a desk and that's all I needed. I set up my books and my laptop and the framed photograph of Joan Didion I'd brought with me. The picture I posted was liked by my mum within seconds, and then nobody else. That was before I realised I could move the outdoor table into the shade and afterwards did all my work in the courtyard. That's where I tanned and typed, under the equatorial sun.

Overlooking the courtyard was the balcony where Papa worked. He invited me up there the first afternoon where he had a similar set-up to me though without books. All he had was a fan and a phone charger fed from a snaking extension cord, and a chair and table with a full ashtray. He offered me cigarettes every time I saw him despite me telling him I'd given up ten years ago. I didn't mind. I was happy to be there and curious about who he was. The first thing I asked him was why he was called Papa and whether that was some kind of Hemingway thing. He laughed and stroked his beard which was white like Hemingway's. I wasn't sure if he understood what I meant. He was the only Afrikaner I had ever met who didn't speak perfect English – at the *plaas* where he grew up, he and his brothers spoke Afrikaans exclusively. I had started learning Swahili on Duolingo and hoped maybe he could help with that. He couldn't. He'd been in Zanzibar for three years and spoke practically nothing.

I realised this on that first afternoon when a young man came out of Papa's room with a handful of plugs and wires. Papa introduced him as Kuku which means *chicken*. Papa thanked him in rusty English and Kuku replied in more proficient English that he would need thirty thousand shillings to fix the light switch in the old man's bathroom. Papa wasn't happy with this and Kuku left with his head down, no money in his hands.

After sharing some tonic water from his fridge, Papa took me across to the beach where the sand glared white and the waves broke a mile out at low tide. The beach was busy with women offering henna, hawkers selling coconuts, Massai in their kangas and Crocs and Oakley sunglasses.

Across the sandflats, women stooped without bending their knees, picking up things from the sand and dropping them into plastic buckets. The hulls of old knackered dhow boats were stripped naked by the sunlight.

Papa pointed down the shoreline where he said there were good hotels, good places to eat, places to meet people. In the distance, the bay curves outwards into the Indian Ocean so that all that is visible of the next village are the kites propelling windsurfers around the headland. He asked if I surfed, said I looked the type. I'm not. I thought perhaps I would snorkel though that's not something I'd ever done either. I had to work mostly. Where better to do it than an island paradise, if only for a few weeks.

Thank God for Zoom, I said to Papa.

He said he understood. I'm not sure he did.

He left me there and after he'd gone the women came to me and tried to sell me henna and massages, while the men – every man who passed – wanted to know where I was from and whether I liked to smoke. There were other white women too, women around my age, walking with Massai boys. The shyness on their faces could not hide their radiant happiness. Their long kanga dresses fluttered around them like the fins of tropical fish. I caught eyes with one and she smiled and lowered her face. Her companion let go of her hand to shake mine.

Karibu, he said, which means *welcome. Karibu sana*, beautiful lady.

Flattery is intoxicating when it comes from beautiful people.

Later, at the guesthouse, Papa was keen to tell me about these women. He told me at length in his pained English that they came from Europe for the *boyfriend experience* and that they paid to sleep with the men. He said the men came across on small boats from the mainland and gave their bodies to these wealthy white women who perhaps really did fall in love, perhaps not. Afterwards, if they got pregnant, the women might stay and marry and set up a business with their husband. Then they would discover that these men were already married to women on the mainland, and that the business was in the man's name only, and then the sad wealthy white women would go back to Europe with their baby.

That's the way Papa told it. I asked him whether he'd seen this happen firsthand and he insisted he had. I felt like he was tinged with that typical racism I had seen before with expats in Africa. He thought that the locals – especially the *mafundi* who built and maintained his guesthouse – were lazy and impractical. Conversely, he also described them as shrewd and scheming. He boasted about how he was building a brand new hotel further down the coast, 'Zanzibar Blue', and how he'd had to install GoPros to make sure the *mafundi* weren't skiving. He even thought of Kuku like that – shy, meek, kind Kuku. I got all of this from my very first conversations with Papa, when he introduced the island as a tropical paradise where things worked at a different pace, on different terms. I thought immediately that these differences had more to do with Papa than anybody else on the island.

Still, it didn't matter to me. I had work to do. I was in Zanzibar to finish writing up a chapter on British colonial history in East Africa. I had a deadline for my publishers that would be no trouble to meet. Papa knew nothing about the British being here, only that *you was everywhere sus*, but he was extremely impressed by my job. He had been a policeman in KwaZulu-Natal and saved enough to retire at the age of fifty, unmarried. Over my first days at the guesthouse he would always pause in the garden where I was working and act amazed, honoured, humbled that someone would choose to write their book in his guesthouse. He asked if he would be in it as a character and I had to repeat almost daily that it was a history book, a commission, a job. He loved horror stories, did I write horror stories? He asked if there was anything he could do for me and I told him about the A/C being broken and the bugs that scratched within the woodwork of my bedframe, but to any request like this he would just shrug and say something like *That's Zanzibar*, and then shuffle off. Sometimes when Kuku was working at the guesthouse I wanted to ask him directly if he could help me with these things. But Kuku was so shy and had such a sharp, quiet intelligence in his eyes I had no desire to treat him how Papa treated him, like a workman, like a lesser. So I made conversation with Kuku whenever he passed through the courtyard, offered him tea and snacks which he always refused. If Papa came onto the balcony when me and Kuku were talking the young man immediately went upstairs to see him. Papa never called down, never said anything, but Kuku would bound up the outer staircase and disappear with him into Papa's rooms, where later the sounds of power-drilling or sanding or the *krik-kruk* of a saw could be heard.

I spent the bulk of my days in the courtyard, sometimes visiting a nearby bar when the building work next door became too loud, sometimes floating in the Indian Ocean and watching the seabirds overhead. In the evenings I would go to the one hotel that, of all the hotels that run in one continuous line ten kilometres up that stretch of the coast, had a regular band playing. I would sit on a crooked stool at the bar watching the musicians play reggae and highlife but never local music. Sometimes they had a hostess named Chichi who would shout *Hakuna Matata* into the microphone between songs. She was from the mainland and wore tiny jean-shorts with the pockets dangling out over her thighs. Tourists took selfies with her often, for which she would spread a generous smile across her face. It was a smile I never saw her use outside of the flash of people's phones but it was real, I think. It was as real as my enthusiasm for my own job, which was most real when I remembered I could be working in Woking or Plaistow or anywhere else but an island in the Indian Ocean. Maybe Chichi felt the same.

One night I asked if she knew Papa but she just lowered her head and returned to the stage without answering. This wasn't the first time I got this reaction when I mentioned where I was staying. At various restaurants and all along the beach, I got the impression that Papa was perhaps disliked, perhaps distrusted. At the locals bar, the only place in the village where the villagers themselves drank, a drunk old man called Papa a *shetani* and then laughed and slapped his cheeks. I left without knowing what he meant, under the gaze of the drunk men and women in that neon blue room, while the giant bats circled over the hotels.

The *shetani* lore was something I didn't take seriously, though Papa insisted that the Zanzibaris believed it wholeheartedly. That was another aspect of his racism – his unquestioning acceptance that these people, while also being practicing Muslims, believed in ghosts and demons and witchdoctors' medicine. He said they performed rituals under the full moon to cast demons out from people, and that blood was involved somehow, blood-letting or blood-drinking. He told me how once the entire village all left their homes during the night and stood waist-deep in the high tide because a *shetani* had been spotted passing through the village in the guise of a tall European man. It was nonsense. The villagers lived in the twenty-first century, just like Papa and the other expats and the tourists and myself. Most of the villagers spoke English, some had been outside of the country. Some had TVs in their houses, others had smartphones. I tried to tell Papa he was talking out of his arse but he just pretended that he couldn't understand what I was saying.

That's Zanzibar, he said, that's Zanzibar, walking away in a hurry while Kuku beat nails into the joists of the balcony.

After a fortnight my work started to flag. I took a trip to Jozani Forest where my bare legs were burnt up by a poisonous plant my guide called 'grandmother's blanket', and afterwards travelled by taxi to the north of the island where the tourist industry has completely consumed the villages of Kendwa and Nungwi. When I returned the next day, I found Papa at the foot of a stepladder, holding it steady for Kuku who was installing security cameras at the guesthouse. Papa seemed embarrassed to be caught doing this but explained it was necessary, very necessary. I had not heard of a single incident of stealing and had been told by several people that burglary was unheard of here. I had received some unwanted attention on the beaches at Kendwa and Nungwi and even in the village but I had rarely felt unsafe. The only people who worried me were the men who drank Konyagi in the middle of the day, though even they were rarely angry or upset. Then there were the tourists who tried to dance with me at the music nights, men who in England I might expect to simply slink off when repelled but who here were entitled, handsy, in holiday-mode. Still, I never felt unsafe, even walking home down the unlit path that leads from the beach to the guesthouse. The darkness there seemed populated only by mosquitoes and ghost crabs and the bats who I had been told do not bite. Regardless, Papa insisted the cameras were needed.

After they were up he and Kuku installed an electric fence that made the guesthouse look like a prison. I asked what he was worried about but he just said *Hakuna Matata, Hakuna Matata*, the same way the Zanzibaris do. One morning I asked Kuku why he thought Papa was so concerned with security but he wouldn't talk to me about it at all. Instead he said that Papa was a *very sensitive man* which I believed because it was Kuku telling me, himself so sensitive. Kuku had already told me that his parents were dead. He was raised by his brothers who worked as *mafundi* in his home village of Makunduchi. I wondered if, beyond my sight, Papa was acting as just that – a father for the young man from Makunduchi who called himself *chicken*.

That night I found Papa drunk at the foot of the staircase, mumbling something about *The Night of the Long Knives*. He blathered on in a mix of Afrikaans and poor English about what will happen the day Mandela dies, how all the black South Africans will rise up and get their revenge for everything that happened. The Night of the Long Knives, the night Mandela dies. I helped him to climb the stairs and unlock his door, explaining over and over that Mandela has been dead for many years.

Around this time I realised I was behind with my chapter but, for whatever reason, the words wouldn't come. The heat rose slowly through December until the strength of the sun was too hard to work beneath, even in the morning. One afternoon, after floating on my back in the ocean, I came across a fisherman casting nets by hand at the shore. His name was Faridi. He was happy I had learnt Swahili – he said I owed him that for me colonising his country, and then he laughed and said *Hakuna Matata*. We spoke as he worked, me with a white towel draped over my head and shoulders, he with his bare skin shining in the sun. Eventually, he held up the tentacles of a dead squid, dripping with seawater and ink. He asked if I wanted to buy it but I emphatically did not.

That afternoon, when Faridi needed a break, we went to a bar and drank Konyagi with tonic water. I asked what he thought of the old *shetani* stories. He laughed and said that they were just that, just stories, but that some of the old people believed them. He remembered when he was young and parts of the island had panicked because a rumour spread that a *shetani* had come over from Pemba. They called this *shetani* 'Popo Bawa', which has something to do with the shadow a bat casts on the ground. I wasn't sure if I was understanding the fisherman's broken English but he seemed to suggest that what people were most afraid of was that Popo Bawa would rape them while they slept. *Pia wanaume*, he said repeatedly, *pia wanaume* – 'also men, also men'. He remembered his father standing guard outside the house all night, waiting for Popo Bawa with a panga in his hand. Faridi's father thought that Popo Bawa had something to do with the Arabs who were massacred during the Revolution but Faridi didn't believe any of it. He wasn't surprised that European expats like me kept these stories going. He said it was just another way to make the Zanzibaris and their traditions look primitive. Faridi knew a limited number of English words but one he knew well was 'savage'.

I asked Faridi whether it was fair to say Papa was unpopular in the village. He said he had to get back to work. So I sat on the sand watching him cast his net in the dusk-light, with the first of the evening's ghost crabs scuttling beside me.

I stopped asking about Papa. But what he told me about prostitution wouldn't leave my mind. I realised there was truth in what he said. I could see it play out while watching the band at the hotel. There were always European women there, dancing with young, slim, bright-eyed Tanzanian boys. There were European men also, who drank with the beautiful women from the mainland. Most of the men were unembarrassed by it but some wouldn't catch my eye. Sometimes the age difference seemed vast – more than thirty years. I had seen the same thing in many countries, wherever poverty and tourism rub up against one another. But I was curious. I didn't get much chance to talk with the prostitutes because they were busy trying to keep the attention of the white people. And besides, what, if any of it, was my business?

One night I asked Chichi whether there was such thing as gay prostitutes but she told me that if there were nobody would ever talk about it. The fact was that it was easy for me to forget, in that island paradise with its cocktails and fireside parties and ubiquitous weed-smells, that homosexuality is punishable by life in prison. I asked Chichi if that applied to lesbians too. It didn't. She said that like Covid-19, the Tanzanian authorities simply didn't believe such a thing existed.

One morning towards Christmas I returned from a trip to the capital to find Papa working with his shirt off in the courtyard. He wore bloody bandages around his arms, knees, torso. I asked him what had happened and he told me he'd fallen on the sharp coral rock that lines the coast on route to Makunduchi. The rocks are sharp, like razors, but I didn't believe him. There was nothing on that part of the island and he never went out just to walk. Men like him didn't walk. For that he would've had to want to soak in the natural beauty of the island, which he never mentioned, or to clear his mind of introspective thought, which he showed no evidence of. I felt sympathy for him, but also a kind of frustration around his willingness to lie to me. He didn't owe me the truth and maybe I shouldn't have expected it. But I did want it. After one month on the island, I was grasping for something I could understand, something real.

I might have asked Kuku if he knew what happened but he didn't show up at the guesthouse for over a week. In his place, I watched Papa tinker with the security cameras all day, and at night sit on the balcony alone and change his bandages while chain-smoking.

I missed home. Not enough to want to be there, but I missed it. I rang my mum and my friends but every conversation made me feel more distant. Things were happening over there, changing, moving on. Less so here. Christmas only took place as a courtesy for the tourists and as an excuse for the hotels to put on more extravagant parties. I didn't see one reindeer, one Santa Claus, one Christmas tree. I didn't hear a single Christmas song. The only evidence that Christmas Day was not exactly like every other day were the Santa hats which the waiters wore in thirty degrees heat. That night I slept with a Danish woman who looked like a young Karen Blixen. I saw her again on New Years' Eve and told her all about Papa and the *shetani* stories and how everyone *hated* him, so I thought, just *hated* him.

Men and their bullshit, she said. Always trouble.

And I laughed her off and kissed her goodbye on the street where a young white man cocked his head at me and smiled like we were there for his pleasure.

Again, it didn't matter. I had my work which was still progressing far too slowly but there was nothing I could do about it. I tried getting up late and working into the evening but the booze was too tempting. I tried waking up early but my brain wouldn't emerge from its predawn fog.

In the mornings, Papa usually drank coffee and smoked cigarettes on the balcony. He never ate breakfast, only swallowed chopped-up pieces of raw garlic which he claimed meant he'd never get malaria. When I thought about this later, I realised this was the only food I'd ever seen him consume. One morning when he was doing his routine I accepted his invitation to join him on the balcony. Kuku was back then and I almost bumped into him on the outer staircase. I tried to ask about where he had been but he was too eager to get past me. When he did I noticed fresh scratches on the back of his neck.

Papa was contemplative that morning. He wanted to tell me about his life. He told me he had once been married but that his wife had abused him and that was one of the reasons he had come to Zanzibar. Another reason was that he had not retired from the police force but was fired for what he called *a misdemeanour* but never described. I wasn't sure what to take from this or why he was telling me but I listened and sympathised and afterwards gave him a hug, our only hug. He said everything would be fine once the Zanzibar Blue hotel got up and running. Construction work was set to finish at the end of February. He said it would change the whole area, change the whole game. He shook my hand again. He held it as if he wanted me to insist that he never let it go.

You are good people, he said, tears in his eyes. *Ja*, good.

I pulled away and tried not to catch his eye again.

Peering over the edge of the balcony, I saw Kuku sitting in the surf, washing his back. He turned his head and saw me looking at him. I pretended to be looking out to sea.

I was too saturated with my work to think through things properly. I regret that now. My deadline was approaching and I knew by early January that I would miss it. That was a double-edged sword. It gave me the freedom to abandon work altogether, at least for a day. Fuck it. I went looking for Papa but he wasn't on his balcony and didn't appear in the afternoon. That was January twelfth, Independence Day, when the islanders celebrate the Revolution. I walked down to where Zanzibar Blue was being built and saw the unfinished stone walls for the first time. I was surprised to see no one working there. On his site and the two half-finished sites adjacent to it on either side, there wasn't a *fundi* in sight. It was getting dark when I walked back. The *dalla dalla* buses were ferrying workers back towards the villages in the north, honking their horns as they passed, men hanging from the back. I heard drumming in the bush between the road and the shoreline. The bats were out in force that night, swooping one after the other in the failing light. When I got back to the guesthouse I walked straight around to where the box for Papa's A/C hung on the outside wall. It was off.

The morning after that new guests arrived and I had to tell them that the owner wasn't around, would probably be back soon, sorry. They waited around all afternoon so eventually I said I would try to let them into Room 5 myself. For all the things he said about the Zanzibaris being slow and lazy, Papa really couldn't be relied on to do anything at all.

That's what made me most angry. He reminded me of landlords in London.

I knew he couldn't have gone far because he hadn't padlocked the door to his office as he usually did. I knocked on the wood until I was sure he wasn't inside and then tried the handle. I called out his name, no answer. I stepped inside.

The keys to Room 5 hung from a hook on the wall, dangling with two dozen others that opened doors to God knows where. At least the guesthouse keys were labelled. Above Papa's desk were a mess of blueprints for Zanzibar Blue. The images showed plans for multiple floors, a dozen rooms or more, balconies, a bar and restaurant area. Underneath the ground floor was another floor, presumably dug out of the coral rock, made up of one large basement room. A bar area was drawn there also, this one with a large dancefloor, as well as a section marked VIP and another marked HOT-TUB/SAUNA. There were small circular platforms with what I guessed were poles for dancing. In the corner, hand-drawn over the original plans in black ink, was what looked like a birdcage. It reminded me of the layout of some of the clubs I had visited with male friends in Brighton and Manchester. How he planned to excavate it from the rock I have no idea.

Below these plans was his desk where I presume he sat and worked whenever he wasn't on the balcony. It was messy and his various ashtrays were all full of yellowed filter tips. There were papers strewn around, financial stuff, and a few photographs of a building site covered with hardcore. In the photographs, *mafundi* posed shirtless among the rubble. The sweat on their bare chests made them shine like polished brass. I opened a drawer. There were more photographs inside, some of *mafundi* on different building sites, some of young men on dancefloors. I recognised one as being inside one of the few nightclubs in Stone Town, a room on the third floor with bent wooden beams that look like they are about to collapse. Papa was in that picture, alone, which made me wonder who took it. Maybe he had friends in the capital after all, people he went to see but that never came here. I still couldn't picture it. I noticed one final photograph in the bottom of the drawer. It was Kuku, two or three years younger than I knew him, fifteen or sixteen years old perhaps. In the picture he stood in front of the guesthouse sign with flecks of paint across his chest. His face is drawn and blank as if he has just been pulled out of a prison camp. I thought of some of the Victorian photographs I had seen at the Anglican Cathedral, photographs from the island's history, the many terrible things that happened then and the other things that happened during the Revolution, the things that nobody spoke about.

44

Kuku's eyes bore into the camera. Not fearful, but hungry.

I gave the new guests their keys for Room 5 and told them Papa would be back any time now. And then I sat in the courtyard as my deadline flew past, not working, wondering what to say to Kuku if he ever returned.

* * *

They found Papa just a few days before I flew home. His body was uncovered by Norwegian tourists among the brush that separates the abandoned southern headland from the road to Makunduchi, just outside the building site for Zanzibar Blue. He was swollen and the insects had got at him so that he was ridden with bites. The police were called and I was amazed that of everyone in the village they asked me to identify him. I demanded to know *why me, for God's sake, I'm a tourist*, but when they asked if I could suggest someone else I realised I couldn't. Maybe I could have asked Faridi or Chichi but that seemed inappropriate too. Kuku still hadn't returned. So I went down to the hospital myself.

The coroner explained the colour of his skin by telling me that his killers had managed to drain about eighty percent of the blood from Papa's body. The coroner told me that while we were still in the room with Papa, still holding the sheet back from his face. I managed to hold it together until I got back to my Airbnb in Stone Town, and then threw up a bellyful of mineral water into the rusted sink.

I finished my chapter on Livingstone in the capital, but before I did I returned just once to the village to be beside the ocean. The guesthouse was closed. The young men looked right through me as if they didn't know who I was. I went to the beach to find Faridi but he wasn't there, and when I saw Chichi at the hotel that night she spoke to me like a stranger.

On the beach, a man tried to sell me a coconut and when I refused sighed *Hakuna Matata*. I remembered the drunken old man who had laughed when he called Papa a *shetani*. Then I saw Kuku, walking in the surf with two older boys either side. I could see even from a reasonable distance that these were his brothers, so alike were they. The only real difference, other than their ages, was the confident walk that made Kuku's sensitive shuffle look even more apprehensive.

They stared at me as they passed, except for Kuku who walked with his head down. I waited for them to stop and say something to me but they said nothing. So I watched them walk away, Kuku in the middle with his head still down, their broad shoulders gleaming in the sunlight.

ANDREW LAURENCE

After The Fall

When the cocktails arrived, Antony had the waiter bring them to their balcony where Carolyn was sitting. It was a routine they would follow every time they stayed in a hotel now, another new element the walking stick propped against the rail beside her, the baton needed to conduct her movement. Before the fall they would dress up and go to the bar to watch the other guests, and amuse themselves making up stories about them, turning them into characters in star-crossed dramas. It was exercise for Carolyn, like playing scales. She was a writer. Antony played whatever game was at hand. Now they wore fat pants and ordered room service and made what they could of the view. This time it was a marina, with fairy lights and yachts and penthouses squatting on apartments, some lit and alive, others dark and deserted.

They raised and touched their glasses in another well-honed routine, begun decades ago on an early date as an ironic nod to the rituals of romance. Exchange a coy look, taste the drink, meet eyes again, raise a brow in appreciation, set down the glass. In the old days, when they'd smoked, he'd light a cigarette for her, parodying forties noir. *Now Voyager.* God, she missed cigarettes.

They studied the harbour searching for mischief.

'See that?' said Antony, nodding to a balcony where light flickered behind a window. 'They're projecting the TV onto the wall. What do you think they're watching?'

'Spiderman?' she suggested. They sipped their drinks and imagined who would enjoy watching a human arachnid crawl across their wall. He said a babysitter and her entitled charges. She imagined a young coder relaxing after a day inventing games of mayhem set in dystopian worlds.

She pointed to a boat secured in the marina, an old yacht, much like one they'd chartered in Greece when they were young and their adventures still physical. Inside the cabin a small screen glinted.

'I wonder if they live on that boat,' she said, pointing.

'Would that be a single or plural they?' Antony asked, showing he could work the new into his thinking, lampooning it in his tone, and puncturing any idea she might have of weaving a romantic tale. His story would be about a man hiding alone, she decided, on the run from his past, rejected or rejecting.

Carolyn searched the horizon for inspiration they could share, and lighted upon the uppermost of the apartments across the marina, a white gabled duplex with floor to ceiling windows stretching the width of its lower level, and open plan rooms brilliant with light. Shapes were flitting across the space.

'What are they doing in that penthouse?' she asked,

'Having a party, I imagine,' said Antony. 'It's Friday.'

'I don't think it's started yet,' said Carolyn. 'They're wearing black. They must be caterers.' Antony nodded. Accept and build, she had taught him, that was the key to creating a story together, as well as a marriage.

'Then that one's the chef,' he said. 'The stationary one. He's making canapes on a kitchen island.'

She leaned forward in her chair, straining to see. They both had cataracts, their sight so blurred what they saw was an interpretation of reality, sometimes an invention. They were due to be fixed soon, and both were excited about this small miracle on the horizon. She could make out two figures in black standing on the balcony, smoking.

'They must have another balcony that faces the river,' she said. 'We're looking into the kitchen. The party will be on the other side.'

'I'm thinking Russian,' Antony said. 'The hosts.'

'Can't be,' said Carolyn. 'They've gone, and their yachts are impounded. Since the war. And these boats are too small for Russians.' Accept and build was all very well, but a story needed a solid foundation. She could tell it stung him, it always did when her observation was keener than his own, it made him feel small, and she could see the suspicion arise in him that it was deliberate.

'Who then?' he asked, sullen now.

'I'd say it's a pied-a-terre, for someone who was something in the City, but is now retired to the country.' She watched as he adjusted to the idea. 'Gus and Cynthia Cotswold.' She always came up with the names.

'Alright,' he said, catching up. 'Old fashioned banker. He bought it years ago off plan. They want to sell it, but the children use it. They have two sons in London, one at the LSE, the other's a musician.'

'Don't forget the daughter,' she said.

'How could I? The clever one. What is she, a brain surgeon?'

'Consultant neurologist,' said Carolyn. 'The youngest in London. They're very proud of her.' One of the catering staff was carrying a box.

'It's her birthday,' said Antony.

'Arabella,' said Carolyn. 'She's thirty-two. The boys are Rufus and Harry. They're younger, and trouble.'

So, the scene was set. It was to be an upmarket family saga, a tale of the rich and spoiled. No cheery cockneys in this story, parodied and patronised for their amusement. This would not be a comedy. They were rarely in the mood for comedy since the fall. They sat in silence with their drinks, watching the sky darken whilst imagining the dramas that might make or break a birthday party.

'What's happening upstairs?' she said, pointing to a window set in the gable, above the caterers, a softly lit room. 'It looks like an office.'

'Could be a sitting room,' said Antony. 'There are two chairs in front of the window, the kind you can relax in.'

'Are those *people* in the chairs?' she asked. They were both craning forwards now, trying to distinguish shapes.

'Looks like it. I could get my glasses,' said Antony. 'I may even have my binoculars.' He often travelled with binoculars, a small pair to look at birds if they were in the country, sometimes just to see, occasionally to pry.

'I think it's the hosts,' said Carolyn. 'They're keeping out of the way, waiting for their guests to arrive. We used to do that.'

'They look like dummies,' said Antony. 'Mannequins, that is, not halfwits.' Carolyn coughed.

'You have no idea why that is so wrong, do you?' she said. 'Maybe they're taking a nap, waiting for the children to turn up.'

'Maybe the children don't want them there,' he said, contrary again.

'OK,' she said, 'maybe they've had a row and fallen out.' She thought of their children and Sunday lunches that had flared into squabbles about school reports or toxic friends, and later, politics, partners, and wasted choices.

'Maybe they're dead,' said Antony, now the highly strung tennis pro, killing the game by smashing the ball into the net.

'What is this now, Stephen King?' Carolyn didn't like horror, or sci-fi, or melodrama, or fantasy, or magical realism, or any stories with a dreamlike quality. She liked her fictional worlds real. That was art. Anyone could twist life into fantasy. Wringing humour, pathos, and eternal truths out of the mundane, now that took talent. In her book characters and story should be possible and set in the present, and in her books they were. It was her way and it had served her well since quitting journalism.

Their attention was distracted by movement on the floor below.

'Are those cocktails?' she asked, making out trays of martini glasses. Antony looked at his watch.

'I imagine the guests are about to arrive,' he said. 'It's about that time.' They watched the scene unfold, eager to see if the evidence supported their hypothesis.

A young crowd arrived glittering in Friday night finery. The caterers glided round the room with drinks and music drifted over to them, a light Latin concoction with a pleasant contralto singing in Italian. It all fit with a birthday party. The hosts upstairs hadn't moved from their seats.

The doorbell rang and Antony glanced at his watch again. It was room service. He opened the door and a waiter wheeled in a trolley, lifted two cloches to reveal a Caesar salad and a hamburger, and opened a bottle of wine. When he was gone, Antony went back to the balcony, stooped, and offered Carolyn his arm, as if inviting her to dance.

She considered the gesture. The arm was strong, but it was a promise of support not intimacy. Was it inevitable that one should give way to the other in the end? She sensed it was given grudgingly. He was frustrated. Who wouldn't be? No one wants their life slowed to a crawl and the fall had slowed his almost as much as hers. She squeezed the gesture for meaning. There was something ironic in it. Forties noir again, the suave hero, or villain, she couldn't say which, offering his arm as a prelude to seduction. But Cary Grant or George Sanders? She'd often wondered which he'd turn out to be. Would he stay or run when the going got tough; save or ruin her in the final reel?

She took his arm with one hand, pushed down on the bone handle of her stick with the other and came to an unsteady verticality. She was an old woman with a stick. It couldn't be. As she gripped his arm she felt a vibration, the tremor he hid but so often betrayed him now. His sign of decline. The little finger on his hand seemed to be waving at her.

He led her inside in the slowest of marches, warning her of the step and handling her like porcelain, until she was seated safely on the sofa. They would eat at the coffee table, using the trolley as a serving cart. He marvelled at how well she was doing and how intrepid they were getting out so soon after the accident, and staying in a hotel, even if it was only a mile or two from the house and only for one night. They were on their way back. He was putting a brave face on it, she knew. The fall had knocked his confidence, undermined his sense of immortality. It was the quality she had loved most about him, but it had seeped away in retirement, with one diagnosis after another, and now her fall. Creeping age was sucking the marrow from his life leaving an exhausted melancholy. He was struggling to find the accept and build in their situation.

How had they arrived at this destination? She wondered. Only yesterday there'd been a gilded youth, a school with a river that ran by it where she'd won prizes, then a university where she'd simultaneously discovered Flaubert, sex, and Germaine Greer, then the exhilaration of London. She was working for a fashion magazine when she discovered Antony at an amateur drama club in Chelsea. He was a dashing young lawyer and a handsome if hammy Horatio in a ludicrous production of Hamlet. She was Ophelia. They became a number at the cast party, thenceforth Tony and Caro, and for a while flirted with the idea of treading the boards. There was a tiny flat in Fulham, a wedding in Kent, then a family in Clapham. This was their golden period, after Antony became known for famous cases, and her first novel was published, and they became sought after guests at dinner parties. They'd had strong nerves, fast metabolisms, and boundless energy, and it seemed their flame was eternal. Antony was asked to preside over enquiries, and she won glittering prizes. They'd had three wonderful acts, was it wrong to want a fourth? Theirs was proving an anti-climax. Overnight, they'd become old and frail. She remembered her mother at eighty-five in a wheelchair, wondering how she'd become so decrepit, and now she understood the look on her face. It was surprise. She'd died quite soon after that, from a fall.

Carolyn looked down at the Ceaser salad. It looked good, enough cheese, the lettuce light and crisp, but she wasn't hungry.

There was a time when it had been a simple game. Stories. It was something she'd always done, and Antony had joined in as part of their courtship ritual. The stories they created then were light, ways of poking fun at the world, while trying to amuse and impress each other. A woman sitting alone at a restaurant table drinking champagne became a secret agent, or a widow who'd murdered her rich husband, or a secretary who'd embezzled the company funds. Later, when their passion had subsided it became a way of debating the world. They gave their characters' jobs and imagined what they had to say about the issues of the day: the cabbie on the Royal Family, the mining baron on global warming, the dinner lady on the Middle Eastern crisis. Then they had children who needed stories and for several years they took turns making up tales about magic, monsters and furry animals, until they weren't wanted anymore, and they started again, just the two of them, in restaurants, on holiday, wherever there were people to watch.

For a long time, it was just one of the things they did, alongside theatre visits and the opera and galleries, and dinner parties, and trips to far flung places. But as they'd aged and roamed less, it had expanded to fill the gaps. Since the fall they'd played cards and watched television until they were numb, when she was in hospital then bedridden at home. Making up stories promised new adventures and needed no physical strength. They didn't even need people to trigger their imaginations anymore. The marina was a luxury.

She toyed with her food as Antony poured the wine. The fall had been an accident, a trip and a slip onto a hard floor, no-one's fault, one of those moment's where life is changed, the world shrunk, and pain enters and refuses to leave. When you were young you recovered from everything, with age it was one damned thing after another, until it sucked you into the earth. She was supposed to be recovering but she wasn't, and this time she feared she wasn't coming back. What would be next, she wondered, what was waiting in the wings to claim her?

Antony cut his hamburger in two and dived into it with enthusiasm. She watched him eat. He still had an appetite. She wondered if he would leave her. She would understand. Their life was turning to stone, hers more quickly than his. He was still handsome, at whatever stage came between Grey Fox and wooden box. He'd find someone.

'I'd understand, you know,' she said, as he ate. 'If you couldn't stand it anymore.' He didn't say anything, just swallowed a mouthful of hamburger. 'If you had to go. It's not much fun for you.'

'Don't be ridiculous,' he said, raising an eyebrow, as if to say, 'And where would I go, exactly?' He was trapped, of course, by duty and guilt and the fear of shame, by a lack of imagination, maybe even by love. It would be easier for everyone if she had died. She wondered if that thought had crossed his mind, and if he'd ever contemplated reaching for a pillow and smothering her while she was asleep. Then he'd be free. They'd both be free.

'I don't want to talk about it,' he said, standing up, his hamburger gone. 'Let's see what's happening at the party.'

He offered her his arm again, brusque this time, and escorted her to the balcony, then returned to collect the remains of the wine. The party had grown raucous. The caterers were clearing plates, two of them skiving on the balcony again; a shimmying huddle behind them suggested dancing. Upstairs the figures in the chairs still hadn't moved.

'Maybe the children killed them,' said Antony.

'Must you turn everything into a third-rate crime drama?' Carolyn asked. 'Are we doing the Menendez brothers now?'

'They shot their parents,' said Antony. 'These poisoned theirs and now they're dancing with the bodies still warm upstairs.'

'Why would they do that?'

'The excitement,' said Antony. 'They're high on cocaine.'

'You'll have Scotland Yard turn up next.'

'They planned it this way,' said Antony. 'They're arrogant. And tonight, after the party they'll dispose of the bodies.'

'Why did they hate them so much?' Carolyn asked.

'They didn't. They just wanted the money. That's enough, these days.' That was his message. This was what the world had come to. Even the Menendez brothers had claimed they were abused.

'Not the girl, though,' said Carolyn, trying to limit the descent into melodrama. 'She had nothing to do with it.'

'If you like.'

'Does it make you feel better?' she asked.

'What?'

'Telling a dark tale.'

Antony frowned. 'Maybe. I don't see a lot of light, these days,' he said.

'My poor baby,' she said. Depression came with his disease.

'You're the poor baby,' he said. He didn't sound convinced. They drank their wine and watched the dancing, lost in separate thoughts.

'Let's go to bed,' she said, at last. 'Or you'll have to go out for cigarettes.'

He rose and presented his arm for the third time, this time a peace offering, and they began the slow march to the bedroom, followed by the undressing, teeth brushing, toilet, medications, and bed, each an arduous process, until they both lay in the dark, listening to the party. She guessed Antony was making his story darker while she weaved a lighter tale to help her sleep, of Arabella showered with gifts and announcing her engagement to howls and applause.

Carolyn woke hours later, needing the toilet, and struggled to sit up, stifling the urge to cry out. The silence was palpable, it was the time before the planes were allowed into Heathrow, before the first birds, before the light. She clawed for her stick, and finding it, heaved herself to her feet, then felt her way to the bathroom in the dark, tracing a path through the unfamiliar space, all the while fearing a fall but refusing to put a light on in case she woke her husband. In the bathroom, when the door was shut, she flooded the room with light and stood blinded in a white marbled oasis.

When she was done, she plunged herself back into darkness, the cavernous black that follows the extinguishing of light, opened the door, and felt her way to the suitcase she knew was on a luggage rack by the wall. Finding it, she lifted the lid and rummaged inside until her hand circled the object she was looking for, then made her way slowly to the balcony, tracing a path on the floor once again, feeling for mines.

The balcony was cool now and the marina dark, the moon hidden behind a cloud. Carolyn sat in her chair, triumphant, and stared at the penthouse. The party was over, the fairy lights out, just a glimmer coming from the window in the gable. She placed her stick against the balcony rail and felt an inexplicable excitement as she raised the binoculars to her eyes, as if a truth was about to be revealed. She trained them on the window and fiddled with the focus wheel, seeking definition. Antony swore they helped with his cataracts, yet however she turned the dial it remained blurry until suddenly there was clarity, and she could see two empty chairs. No shapes, no figures, no mannikins. Behind them someone was hoovering. She couldn't be sure who.

She lowered the binoculars, trying to imagine a narrative, and noticed a suggestion of movement below the gable on the ground floor, outside on the pavement. She trained the binoculars again and fiddled with the focus wheel until she saw the car, a black SUV with the rear hatch open. Two men were tossing black bin liners into the back, while casting glances round the marina. They were young and smartly dressed. The sons, Carolyn decided. She puzzled why they would be taking out rubbish when the party had been professionally catered, then watched as they disappeared behind a door, and reappeared moments later, struggling with a bigger, heavier bag, a wheeled duffle, and loaded it into the SUV. They repeated the exercise with a second bag. She watched as one shut the rear door while the other climbed in and started the engine. They drove away without lights. She looked up and caught the silhouette of a woman looking down from the upper window. The woman turned into the room and switched off the light, after which the marina was at peace again.

She puzzled over what she had seen. It was just a story. They had made it up. It hadn't been real. She sought an innocent explanation to support the facts, a mundane reality, but couldn't find one. Antony had made the story up and it had come true. What were the odds on that? The idea occurred to her that the stories they made up always came true, that they altered reality somehow, like the plot of some cheap sci-fi novel; then she imagined that Antony knew them somehow, the killers, knew what was going to happen, was staying at the hotel to supervise the murder, some twisted mentor and lookout, on a percentage. And he'd used the tale to score points in their game, unable to resist the temptation to tell a tale he knew was true. But that would make her a witness to a terrible crime, wouldn't it? And Antony a murderer. This was ridiculous. She reached for her stick. It was a silly game and getting out of hand. She should stop. They were just fears and ideas they turned into stories, wild guesses and exaggerations that became fictions, and yes, occasionally they came close to the truth. There would be a simple explanation for what she had seen. And what had she seen? Had she even seen what she thought she'd seen? She couldn't trust her eyes anymore. Or could it be the medication? She'd had all sorts of paranoid fantasies in hospital, even imagining a conspiracy where her ward was used for unscheduled operations in the middle of the night, transplanting organs stolen from patients into Russians for hard cash. Had she taken the strong pill tonight? The opiate? The one that had brought America to its knees that she'd been surprised to find was still prescribed. The Sackler one. Antony had supervised her medications. This was all too absurd. It was time to find an ending.

She heard a sound behind her, the sliding of a drape along a track, and turned to see Antony stepping onto the balcony, dressed in a fluffy white bathrobe, clutching a pillow in trembling hands, moving slowly towards her. He looked sorrowful but determined.

'You got out of bed,' he said, the pillow in front of him.

'Oh, Antony,' she sighed. Not this ending. Please no. She tried to imagine her last words and whether she would struggle.

'I thought you might find it more comfortable,' he said. 'To sit on.' He placed the pillow on the other seat, his, and plumped it. Then he held out a hand. In his palm were two pills. 'Paracetamol,' he said. He offered an arm to transfer her from one chair to the other.

She smiled. So, this was the twist. Of course, it was. He was Cary Grant after all, not a cad, but a kind and patient man who had decided to accept and build. It was a reassuringly mundane reality and mundane was usually true. There had been no shapes in chairs. The party could have been anyone's. The bags were luggage, the men on the way to the airport for an early flight, the woman a watchful wife. She looked across the marina to the penthouse which was lightening as the day began to break.

She was a storyteller, she reminded herself, not a witness.

T.N. EYER

The Offer

The building is in an office park along the freeway. It is six stories tall with ample parking and a warm yellow sign extending into the sky. *High Quality Life* the sign reads in black cursive. Dolores Montague has passed it every day on her commute for years. She knows what kind of work they do, and she has thought many times that she's glad it exists, that it's good for people to have options, but *she* would never take that option. Except now she is.

She exits the freeway and follows the signs toward High Quality Life. The closer she gets, the faster her heart beats, and the faster her heart beats, the more she accelerates, until she is zooming down the road. Now that she has made this decision, she is eager to put her plans in motion. She hopes her certainty comes through in the interview. She has heard that any hesitation could be held against her, that a tremor in her voice or a quiver in her hands could doom her case. And that can't happen. She needs this to work out.

Dolores parks directly in front of High Quality Life's door. She says out loud, "I'm Dolores Montague, and I'd like to meet with an Opportunity Specialist." She is relieved that she sounds as resolved as she feels.

She takes a deep breath, and then gets out of the car and strides toward the entrance like this is any old errand. Low stakes. Mundane.

The lobby reminds her of an elementary school with bright furniture and smiling employees. She half expects to find children's indecipherable artwork Scotch taped to the walls.

The receptionist, a slender fellow in his twenties wearing a boyish dinosaur tie, greets her warmly. "How can I help you today?"

"I'm Dolores Montague, and I'd like to meet with an Opportunity Specialist," she recites. She had planned to smile, but now she fears it would look forced. Smiling has never come naturally to her.

"Of course," the boy says. "Do you have an appointment?"

An appointment? It had not occurred to Dolores that she needed one. Did people schedule this kind of thing the way they booked theater tickets or reserved a hotel room? "No," she says. "I don't have an appointment."

She is kicking herself. Not having an appointment probably makes this visit seem less carefully considered, and they want carefully considered, she knows they do.

"No problem," the receptionist says, still smiling at her. "If you'll have a seat in the waiting area, someone will be with you shortly." He gestures toward a circular space a few feet away from the reception desk, with curved red couches and a round orange table atop a sun-shaped yellow rug.

Dolores thanks him and sits in the center of one of the couches to discourage anyone from sitting next to her. Not that anyone would. She is the only person in the waiting room, though the building as a whole feels buzzy, busy. There are a lot of people walking around, talking to each other and into their phones. She sees a large woman in her fifties or sixties walking toward the exit with a frail man in his eighties at least. "The money will be direct deposited within seventy-two hours," the woman is saying as she extends her hand toward the man. "Congratulations, Mr. Thomas."

Seventy-two hours, Dolores thinks. That fast? Incredible. In seventy-two hours she could be a millionaire. Mr. Thomas thanks the large woman and makes his way toward the door, slow but steady, the opposite, Dolores thinks, of her two-year-old grandson, who runs as fast as he can until he stumbles or slips or crashes into something with a bang.

Dolores feels heartened by the exchange between Mr. Thomas and the Opportunity Specialist. She shifts from butt-cheek to butt-cheek in her excitement. She is a boxer before a bout, her anxiety giving way to an adrenaline-fueled energy that she knows will propel her to success. If only her Opportunity Specialist would come!

To keep herself in the right headspace, Dolores silently rehearses what she will say. Her speech, she knows, must strike a careful balance. She must be purposeful but not desperate. Sympathetic but not weepy. Omissions are okay but not outright lies. There's a background check, after all, though she's not sure what it entails.

"Ms. Montague?"

Dolores looks up. A young, pretty girl, with short curly hair and red-rimmed, cat's eye glasses is smiling at her. She has paired a chunk red sweater with a yellow pleated skirt that, in Dolores's opinion, is a tad too short to be professional.

"Yes?" Dolores says, urging her lips up into a smile.

"I'm Samantha, your Opportunity Specialist."

Oh, god, of course she is. Dolores wants to ask if she can have the older woman who had just worked with Mr. Thomas instead. She cannot imagine describing her pathetic life to someone as young and starry-eyed as this.

"Do you want to follow me?" Samantha asks.

Dolores springs from her seat. "Yes, of course," she says. She should have gotten up as soon as Samantha said her name. She'll have to hope her hesitation came across as confusion, not uncertainty. There can be no uncertainty.

Samantha's office, like the rest of the building, like Samantha herself, is decorated in primary colors. Samantha settles in behind her desk, still smiling. Dolores takes one of two chairs facing her, trying to match Samantha's brightness with a beaming grin of her own. It makes the sides of her mouth hurt.

"How can I help you?" Samantha asks, pulling a notepad and pen from her desk drawer.

Dolores reaches into her enormous pleather tote bag, extracts a thin folder, and sets it on Samantha's desk. "I've been diagnosed with a terminal disease, and I'd like to talk about my options."

She had read somewhere that 'I'd like to talk about my options' was received more positively than 'I'd like an Offer.'

Samantha's smile becomes a look of genuine concern. "I'm so sorry," she says, but she doesn't reach for the folder. "Do you want to tell me more about it?"

Dolores isn't prepared for this. She wants to tell Samantha the folder has all the information she needs, but she suspects this wouldn't go over well. "It's cancer," Dolores says, downplaying the diagnosis with a little shrug. "Stage 4. The doctors think they can keep me alive for five or six years with chemo, but it's already spread, so, there's only so much they can do."

Dolores had been unsurprised when the doctor delivered the news. "That figures," she'd said, referring both to the cancer and to the fact that it was incurable. That was how things went in her life, from bad to worse.

"And how does that make you feel?" Samantha asks, leaning forward and picking up the pen.

Dolores's attempts at happy falter. "How do you think it makes me feel?" she snaps. "Crappy. It's a crappy thing to know you'll be dead by sixty-five."

"I'm sorry," Samantha says. "Of course it is."

Dolores takes a deep breath, angry at herself for losing control. "I'm sorry I snapped at you," she mutters, wondering if her case is already sunk.

"It's okay," Samantha says, but her voice is icy. "Let me walk you through how this process works. I'm a Level One Opportunity Specialist, or a screener. My job is to see how you're doing, what headspace you're in, why you decided to come and see us today, that kind of thing. Assuming everything looks good and you want to proceed, I'll pass you on to a Level Two Opportunity Specialist, who will help you submit an application to your insurance company for an Offer. Does that sound okay?"

"Fine," Dolores says, even though it sounds like a lot of bureaucratic hoopla to her.

"May I ask, what's your prognosis without chemo?"

"Three years tops." Her voice cracks despite her effort to sound matter-of-fact.

Samantha's sympathetic frown twists, and her lower lip pouts out. Her mouth looks like a croissant, Dolores thinks.

"Before we go forward, I want you to know there's nothing wrong with fighting even if you know you'll ultimately lose," Samantha tells her.

Dolores freezes. Well shit, she thinks. This is what she'd been afraid of, some twenty-two-year-old sending her away because she doesn't understand that you can be sad about a decision and still know it's what's best for you.

"I believe in picking my battles," Dolores says, crossing her arms. "And as much as I'd like to live, this isn't one I'm interested in fighting. The cost is too great."

Samantha is taking notes as Dolores talks. "The cost to whom?" she asks.

Dolores knows she is imagining pushy relatives, worried about medical expenses or their dwindling inheritance, burdened by the mere thought of having to take care of a bedridden old fogey. Dolores decides to set her straight. "The cost to myself," she says. "You think chemo sounds like fun? You think spending the last years of my life vomiting and losing my hair interests me? No, thank you. If I only have a few years left, I want to enjoy them."

She sees Samantha nod almost imperceptibly, and she knows this is what the girl wanted to hear. "Of course. We're very sympathetic to quality of life claims here." She glances down at her notes. "And when did you receive your diagnosis?"

"Two weeks ago tomorrow," Dolores says. She expects the next question to be *What have you been doing since?* And then she will smile meekly and say she has been contemplating what she wants the rest of her life to look like when the truth is the past two weeks have looked no different from any other. Her children – Jessica, 33, and Benji, 31 – are drowning. No, that is an understatement. Her children are cannon balls dropped into a bathtub. They have hit rock bottom with unexpected speed and force, and she is trying desperately to pick them up again, but they are not only extremely heavy they are slippery when wet. And maybe, just maybe, the sad truth is she'd rather throw money at their problems than continue to try to save them herself. Write them checks and then sail off into the sunset. Yes, that's what she wants. Not that she'd ever admit that to them or to Samantha or to anyone else for that matter.

Mercifully Samantha just smiles and nods. "That's good," she says. "You've had time to think things through. Sometimes people come to us straight from the doctor's. They aren't in the right headspace. They're too distraught. Like any of us would be."

She blushes and amends, "Like you probably were two weeks ago. Anyway, we don't accept or reject them. We don't even consider their cases then. We tell them to go home, sleep on it, and come see us in a few days. One week, that's the minimum time between diagnosis and when we'll first consider a case. We want to give everyone time to process the news. Talk about it with their families. Have you, by the way? Talked about it with your family?"

Dolores, who had been placidly nodding along as Samantha spoke, now feels as though Samantha has snapped her neck. Her family? Does Samantha mean her kids? Well, no. She hasn't talked to them. "Yes," she says. "I have."

"And?" Samantha is leaning toward Dolores like a therapist anticipating a breakthrough. Dolores gazes at her wearily, as she tries to mix a three-ingredient cocktail that is at once believable, close enough to the truth that Dolores will remember it, and what Samantha wants to hear. How *would* her son and daughter react?

"Well," Dolores begins, "They were upset. My daughter cried. She's trying to have a baby, and it makes her sad to think I won't be around to watch her child grow up. That makes me sad, too, obviously." Kind of. Honestly, helping with Benji's son has reminded her of what a pain in the ass kids can be.

"My son, well, he was sad, too, but he also has a lot going on right now, and I feel like my news was the straw that broke the camel's back. He kept saying things like, 'Great. This is just what I need.' To be honest, I kind of regret telling him." That's exactly how Benji would react. She knows it. It's why she hasn't told him. It is more than he can handle. It would break him. Or at the very least send him on another bender.

"So both of your children thought of your terminal disease in terms of its impact on them. How does that make you feel?"

"Is this a therapy session?" Dolores asks, grumpy now. She doesn't want to talk through her feelings. She wants an Offer.

"No," Samantha says. "But it is important to me that you're making this decision because it's what you want, not because you worry about being a burden to your children."

"I wouldn't be a burden to my children," Dolores says. "I couldn't be. They won't take care of me when I get sick, whether it's from the chemo or the cancer. They have too much on their plates. They're too self-absorbed."

She has thought about this already. Benji would text meaningless one-line messages every few days. 'Thinking of u.' Or 'How r u mom?' But he'd never call or come to see her. Jessica would stop by with tubs of store-bought soup, leave them outside Dolores's door, then text to let her know they're there, saying she's sorry she couldn't come in, but her husband has to jab her in the ass in the next five minutes or they'll never have a baby. If Dolores asked them to pick up a prescription or drive her home from the hospital, they would talk about how much they wanted to, if only…If only Benji didn't have his wife and daughter to take care of. If only hospitals didn't stress Jessica out.

Samantha's face has pinched and contracted as though she smells something foul. As though Dolores has farted in her office. "You'd be surprised," she says. "Family can really step up when it matters."

Dolores knows she should probably say something nice and agreeable, but instead she rolls her eyes. Samanatha's saccharine comments are getting on her nerves. "You don't know my kids," she says. "I love them, but they don't have the capacity for that right now. My daughter's fertility struggles are expensive and all-consuming. My son has a wife who can't hold down a job, a son who's been kicked out of two daycares already, and an alcohol problem. They were both upset when I told them I had cancer – really, genuinely upset – but neither of them offered to help. Neither of them said they'd be there for me. And they were right not to, because it would have been a lie. There's a limit to how much they can do."

"I'm sorry," Samantha says. "You're right. It was presumptuous of me to suggest that I know your family better than you do. But I have to ask, are your kids influencing your decision to seek an Offer?"

The right answer is 'no', Dolores knows it. But before she can stop herself, she is saying, "Well, of course they are. And so is my financial situation. And my job's medical leave policy. And the fact that I don't have a partner. And my fear of chemotherapy and sickness more generally. Lucky for me all of these factors point to the same solution: I want an

Offer. I don't want to suffer. I want to enjoy the time I have left, and then, when my health takes a turn, I want all the comfort drugs I can get until I die."

Samantha looks visibly uncomfortable. She thumbs through her notepad and nibbles on her pen cap. Then she stands abruptly. "Excuse me," she says, as she hurries from the room.

Well shit, thinks Dolores. I've blown my only shot. She wonders if they'll let her come back next month and try again.

Dolores looks around Samantha's office, her leg shaking the way it does when she's agitated. There are two prints side-by-side on the wall – a vibrant drawing of the sun rising on the left, and an equally vibrant drawing of the sun setting on the right. They are both colorful, optimistic. As though Samantha believes that life can be equally beautiful at its beginning and at its end. Hogwash, Dolores thinks. The beginning of life is all promise, the end, all disappointment and regret. She doesn't think an Offer will rectify that, but it would give her the chance to do some of the things on her bucket list (travel, mostly), and it would spare her from the suffocating monotony of her daily life, a life she had gotten stuck with years ago, not one she had ever wanted.

A sour taste rises from Dolores's throat, and her chest heaves up and down as she breathes slow, heavy breaths. She is angry all of a sudden. Brow furrowing, fist clenching furious. Why should this twenty-two-year-old have any effect on what happens with the rest of Dolores's life? What does she know about when someone should live or die? Why does she get to determine if someone is making this decision for the right reasons or the wrong ones? This is horse shit. She will demand to speak with Samantha's supervisor, make her arguments to someone of a more reasonable age.

But then Samantha returns with a middle-aged man. He is slender with kind eyes, hidden behind wire-rimmed glasses. His clothes are not abrasively bright but sensible and grey. He looks like an adult.

"Ms. Montague?" he says. He has a therapist's voice. Dolores bets he is a therapist, and she fears, suddenly that her answers were so bad that Samantha has recommended counseling instead of submitting her request for an Offer.

"Yes?" Dolores says, irked.

"My name is Mark Watchtower. I'm a Level Two Opportunity Specialist. My job is to help you with your application for an Offer."

"My application?" she says. "Does that mean I passed?" If so, why hadn't Samantha told her that instead of running from the room like she was afraid for her life?

"It's not really a pass/fail process," Samantha says. "It's a check, to make sure this is what you really want."

"If I didn't want it, would I be here?" Dolores tries – and fails – to keep the irritation from her voice.

"The elderly can be vulnerable," Samantha says, smiling benevolently. "We have to make sure you're not the victim of elder abuse or coercion."

"That's not infantilizing at all." She needs to get out of this office. Her temper flares when she feels insulted. She can't resist the urge to snap back. This has twice gotten her put on probation at work and once resulted in her being denied a promotion. Her daughter says she should try yoga, but she can't imagine having the time to sit around and 'clear her mind' for more than about ten seconds.

Samantha is blushing and stuttering, looking for a way to backtrack probably. Mark intercedes. "It is infantilizing and frankly, frustrating. This is your choice to make, not ours. Unfortunately, it's also protocol."

"Of course it is," Dolores grumbles, but already she likes Mark better than Samantha.

"Regardless, there were no red flags in your case," Mark tells her.

Samantha is nodding enthusiastically as though she's eager to be back in Dolores's good graces. "You're a spitfire," she says. "No way anyone is convincing you to do something against your will."

"No," Dolores agrees. She suspects now that what she had said to Samantha mattered less than how she'd said it.

"Why don't we go to my office and complete your application, Ms. Montague?" Mark says.

Now that she has gotten what she wants and conciliatory gestures have been made, the fire within Dolores becomes embers, then ashes. "Sure," she says. "Thank you for your time, Samantha."

Samantha seems startled by her sudden politeness. "Of course, Ms. Montague."

Dolores follows Mark out of Samantha's office and down the hall. "What percentage of the people who come in here are being coerced anyway?"

He smiles. "Less than one percent," he says. "But between you and me, that's not the real reason for those screenings."

"Oh?" She steps up to walk beside him.

He glances over at her. "It's the lawyers, the lawsuits."

"Lawsuits?"

"Sure. Imagine we have someone like you – sixty-two years old with a terminal cancer diagnosis. This person agrees to forego chemotherapy and instead receive a lump sum of half a million dollars and unlimited palliative care. A year later, he changes his mind. Now, he wants chemo. He wants to fight."

"Well, that's tough," Dolores says. "He took the payout. You can't have your cake and eat it, too."

Mark seems amused by her. "Well, let's change the scenario a little. Imagine a man decides he wants to commit suicide, so he jumps off a bridge. If you see him flailing around in the sea, and it's within your power to save him, are you going to let him drown?"

"No," she admits. "Not if there's no risk to me."

"So what do we do when somebody accepts an Offer and then changes their mind a year or two later? Leave them to drown?"

"That is a quandary," she says. "I guess they'd have to pay back the money, and then they get treatment."

"And if they can't?"

"How do you go through half a million dollars in a year?" she marvels. "Well, then, I guess they'd have to pay for it out of pocket."

"When a person accepts an Offer, that's exactly what the contract provides. They can still receive treatment, but their insurer is not liable for the cost of care."

"So that's that then."

"A lot of people disagree with you. There's an onslaught of lawsuits, a slew of angry patients and devastated family members, all claiming that denying care is unconscionable."

"People need to learn to live with the consequences of their actions," Dolores proclaims, frustrated. But even as she is saying it, she can imagine her kids accepting Offers, spending the money, and then demanding to receive treatment anyway. Entitled, that entire generation.

"People make mistakes," Mark says. "And denying them medical coverage is a harsh punishment for that. That's why we try to make sure our clients are certain before we help them solicit an Offer. And it works. Since we implemented that first round of screening, the number of people wanting treatment after accepting an Offer has plummeted."

They are in Mark's office now. Like everything else in this building, it looks like it belongs to a kindergarten teacher, but at least the art – a vintage map of San Francisco with all the landmarks labeled – is less on the nose.

"Why can't I fill out this application myself?" Dolores asks, settling into the seat closest to the door.

"Because I'm better at it," Mark says, smiling at her. Dolores can't decide whether she finds him confident or cocky. She squelches the urge to argue with him.

"Fine," she says. "Tell me what you need to know."

He asks for her driver's license, and she watches as he fills in a form on his computer: her name and birthdate, her contact information.

"What do you do for a living?" he asks.

"I work at the DMV. Does that surprise you?" It never surprises anyone.

He emits a low whistle, an 'I don't envy you' whistle. "It takes a strong person to do a job like that."

She cocks her head at him. She has never heard this take on her job before. "Well, yes," she says. "Yes, it does. People can be such assholes."

He nods. "And your salary there?"

She raises her eyebrows. "Now why do you need to know that?"

He turns away from the computer and toward her, crossing his fingers and resting his hands on his desk. "What do you think is the point of this application?"

His voice is kind, paternal. It's the therapist voice again. "To get me an Offer," she says. She doesn't add 'obviously' even though she wants to.

"Sure," he says. "But the insurance company doesn't just say 'Yes, this person deserves an Offer' or 'No, this person doesn't.' They have to decide how much they're willing to give you."

Dolores considers this. She has to admit, she's never thought about how they calculate the dollar amount. She'd assumed there was some chart or equation, that her information was simply plugged in and a number was spit out. "So your job is to convince them to give me more?"

Mark's lips disappear into his mouth as he considers this. "This isn't an adversarial process," he says eventually. "It's not us versus the insurance company. Rather, we all work together to arrive at an Offer that's fair to everybody. For that to happen, we need more information."

She decides to accept this for now, though she is skeptical. It seems to her the fairest thing would be an equation.

She tells Mark how much she makes. Her salary is mid-five figures, which would be more than enough if her kids would stop asking for money, but her benefits are substantial. She makes a point of mentioning this to Mark, who nods. "Oh, I know," he assures her. "That's the best part of working for the government."

"Do you have a partner?" he asks.

"No," she says. "That asshole left when the kids were still babies. Came home from work one night, looked around at the messy house and the screaming kids and me covered in sick, and started packing his belongings in a trash bag. When I asked what he was doing he said, get this, 'This isn't the life I dreamed of'. As if that matters. As if my dream

was to be abandoned by my husband and left to raise two kids by myself."
She cannot think of her ex-husband without getting worked up. She will
never forgive him for leaving her to fend for herself. He never sent child
support either, just divorce papers, the places for her to sign marked with
neon green Post-its.

"I'm sorry," Mark says.

She wishes she could tell him not to worry about it, that it's water under
the bridge, but the truth is, it had ruined her life. She'd had to drop out of
college, get that shitty job at the DMV. Work all day and then go home to
two small kids. She hadn't ever had time for herself after that. It had been
all work, all the time. She had lost her friends and her hobbies. She'd
grown bottom-heavy from sitting behind a desk all day.

"Now you understand why I want an Offer," she huffs. "With a little
cash, I can do something for me, for a change."

She has already thought about what she will do with the money.
Twenty-five thousand to each of her children – about twenty-four
thousand more than either of them ever has in the bank– and the rest she'll
spend on cruises. Cruises to Alaska and the Caribbean and around Europe,
maybe even Asia and the South Pacific. One cruise after another until she
dies or the money runs out. If the latter, well, she'll use the palliative
morphine they prescribe to end it herself. Or maybe just jump overboard,
though that seems a tad dramatic to her.

"I get it," Mark says, and she suspects that he does.

He asks more questions. She tells him about her kids – the same stories
she'd told Samantha. She discloses her financial assets and liabilities – an
outstanding mortgage on a double-wide in a trailer park but no other
liabilities, or assets for that matter. About three thousand dollars in the
bank. A pension plan. He asks about her health next, but she doesn't have
any co-morbidities. She doesn't smoke even though everyone else at the
DMV does. Drinks socially – by which she means at home by herself but
only one or two a night. She's a little overweight but nothing too serious,
and while she doesn't technically exercise, she'd estimate she walks at
least a mile five times a week. Mark types away on his computer, the keys
clacking rhythmically. Dolores keeps her eyes on his screen, making sure
what he writes is accurate, but there's no need to worry. He's a faithful
scribe.

When he is done, he spins the screen toward her. "Look it over," he
says. "Make sure you're happy."

It is her life, reduced to four pages. As she reads through it, a funny
thing happens. She starts to cry. "It isn't much, is it?" she mumbles.

He passes her a tissue. "You have done right by everyone in your life," he tells her. "You raised your children. You worked hard. You didn't complain or become a burden to anyone. You've done enough."

He pauses then repeats, "It's enough."

Her muscles, which have been taut for years, begin to relax. She realizes she has been waiting her whole life for someone to tell her this. "Thank you," she says.

"I mean it." He glances at the screen, at her application. "I'll submit this for you. My guess is your Offer will be around $400,000, but we should hear from the insurance company within the next thirty days. Once we do, it's up to you – accept their Offer or decline it."

"Extend my life or enjoy it, you mean."

He gives her a sad smile. "I wish it could be both."

She shrugs. She is no-nonsense again. Tough-as-nails. "Life is full of trade-offs," she says. "I'm okay with this being one of mine."

HOUSSAM ALISSA

The Second Coming

When Jesus finally did return, he chose to stage his earthly comeback outside the Iceland on New Malden High Street, for reasons that were never made clear.

"The Kingdom of God is nigh," he cried out to the shoppers of south-west London. "Repent your sins and enter your Father's Love."

It was a Saturday, and people were trying to get into Poundland. A woman in an African headwrap with bags in each hand kissed her teeth irritably at the Lord as he blocked her path to tell her He loved her.

The Son of God wore white robes, crudely cut and raw-seamed; like a child's nativity costume stitched together the night before from old bedsheets. His skin was pockmarked and his beard scraggly; mousey, unshampooed hair frizzed down to his shoulders. His fingers were long and thin and skeletal and he had big, kind green eyes, like an anime character.

"Confirmed: Jesus *is* in fact white," Saima remarked as we passed him coming out of the mini-Tesco on our lunch break one Wednesday, adding this finding to her Instagram stories. At the time we were both working at the local Curries.

"And an AC-DC fan apparently," I said, noticing the tattoo on his wrist. We watched him preach as we ate our meal-deals on the iron bench across the street from the Iceland.

At first Jesus was just being generic Jesus. School Assembly Jesus. Telling us to love and forgive one another, to feed the hungry, to repent our sins (Saima: "I thought he *died* for our sins so we didn't have to though? Isn't that like the whole point of him?") etc. All the cozy Jesusy stuff your grandma is into. Nobody took him especially seriously. The odd person stopped to chat with him. Others even tossed him the odd coin, for which he would bow his head in thanks. Yet more people shook their heads and made wisecracks to each other. But mostly, people ignored him.

Then one week Jesus changed tack.

First he spoke out against the Royals, amid the growing scandal on the front pages. He referred to them as a 'brood of vipers', 'preying upon the flesh of the meek'.

"A tree is known by its fruit," he declared. "And I tell you, this tree is rotten."

This got him a few chuckles and bemused shakes of the head. He got even more attention when he set fire to a ten-pound note, burning the Queen's effigy.

"There is but one King," he declared solemnly as Lilabet blackened and curled. "And His is the Kingdom of Heaven."

"*My* guy," Saima breathed, little red hearts practically bubbling up over her head.

Not a week later, he went after the branch of N— Bank; loudly proclaiming them to be a 'den of thieves' who had 'crippled the economy with their greed', leaving 'millions ruined and hungry.'

"Not inaccurate," Saima pointed out, one of many in the gathered crowd filming the ensuing debacle on her phone as the branch manager, an exasperated Sikh man whose nametag read DAVINDER, threatened to call the police on the Son of God if he didn't stop 'harassing' customers. But the customers appeared to be loving it.

"Tell them to stop sending me threatening letters," one ruddy-faced old man shouted out as Jesus stood aloft a recycling bin to heap damnation upon the 'corpulent priests of commerce'. Cheers went up when the Lord referred to the mortgage system as an 'unholy abomination' and called for the forgiveness of all debts, poor Davinder pacing frantically below with his phone pressed to his ear.

This was not your grandma's Jesus. This was rabble-rousing, table-flipping, I-came-not-to-bring-peace-but-the-sword Jesus. The Messiah was back, baby.

Eventually, as they do, the police showed up to poop the party. The crowd was dispersed amid boos and the Saviour was let off with a warning.

"Jesus got cancelled," Saima sighed, adding the caption to her reel.

"To be fair the Romans literally crucified him," I said, rolling a cigarette. "Difficult to get more cancelled than that."

The Messiah was subsequently seen popping into Greggs for a sausage roll, but not before he had his selfie taken with several of the standers-by and was even asked for an autograph. He laid low for a while after that, disappearing from the High Street for a week or two following the bank stunt.

When Jesus came back, he came back to denounce violence.

"They are butchering my Children," he cried out in anguished tones. Somehow, from somewhere, he had procured a photo of massacred Middle Eastern children blown up onto an A2 placard, which he held aloft on the High Street. Reviews of this were mixed. Many an angry mother stopped to chide him for the graphic display, and one dad threatened to 'fucking slap' Jesus if he didn't put it away. Conversely, the Good Shepherd received a warmer reception from the Kingston Uni students who lived in the area and won himself the respect of New Malden's Arab community, receiving from them a number of solemnly approving nods, a couple of fist bumps, and one "YES BROTHER JESUS" screamed out from the window of a souped-up Nissan Micra blasting 90s hip-hop and reeking of weed. Naturally it didn't take long for the police to show up again. This time they confiscated the placard, which Jesus swiftly replaced with a flag (again, no idea where he got it from). But after a few days of waving the flag in solidarity with the genocided, Jesus got real again.

"Their profits," he announced outside a major UK supermarket. "Are paying for bombs that kill babies. Their oranges are *blood* oranges. This is no supermarket, but a butcher's." He was speaking through a megaphone (no clue) and had a printed stack of fliers with the image of the dead children, headed: MURDER. He stuck one to the window of the supermarket, and as the fed-up-with-life security guard waddled over to remove it, he slapped on a few others for good measure.

Trailing a handful of filming onlookers, Jesus made his march down the high street slapping the fliers onto select shop and restaurant windows, while his tiny crowd of followers chanted "Butchers! Butchers!"

"Ooo let's follow them!" Saima gasped, clutching my arm. We weren't even on a break this time, we had dashed work just to watch the furore unfold.

Jesus probably managed to get halfway down the High Street before, with a flash of blue lights and a blast of siren, the bobbies showed up. This time they handcuffed the Lord and bundled him in the back of their squad car, driving him away amid booing. The Son of God went quietly and without a fight, which seemed on-brand for him.

Saima's video of the arrest went semi-viral, and even made it onto the Surrey Comet's website (VIDEO SHOWS 'JESUS' ARRESTED IN NEW MALDEN). The comments were a predictable bin-fire, until the Comet disabled them.

For a long time after that, there was no sign of the Messiah.

"I reckon he went back up to heaven innit," Saima asked as we reset the laptop displays.

"I wouldn't blame him," I said. "Earth is fairly shit."

"I hope they didn't put him in jail."

I shrugged. "He's been through worse, I suppose." I thought about Jesus standing at the dock in a magistrate's court, with his robes and friendly Studio Ghibli eyes, having his crimes read out to him by the clerk of the court.

"Did he actually do anything wrong? I swear he didn't though." She hammered at the keys of a netbook stuck on bluescreen.

"Not wrong," I said. "Possibly illegal."

"'Disturbing the peace'," Saima suggested. "My brother says they always bang man up for that when they got nothing else."

"Maybe. Or maybe he's just going through the system, homeless services or whatever."

"Was he even homeless?"

"I have no idea. He clearly had access to resources of some kind. Maybe it's a psychiatric thing, I don't know."

"I don't think he's *crazy*."

"I didn't say 'crazy'."

"Like saying killing children is bad isn't crazy." "I completely agree. But thinking you're Jesus is, a bit, maybe?"

"Unless you *are* Jesus. Anyway I hope he comes back," Saima said, giving up on the netbook and fixing her headscarf. "He got me bare followers."

*   *   *

Every English town seems to have a local eccentric that brings character to the community. The alcoholic who dresses up like a beefeater. The wizard who walks his ferrets on leashes. The guy who cycles around with coloured strobe-lights and a boombox blasting reggae attached to his bike. Ours was Jesus Christ, Son of God and Saviour of Humanity. By the time of his arrest, he even had a little Facebook group dedicated to him and was regularly featuring on the NextDoor app. So when the police took him away, the High Street felt empty without him, lonely, somehow.

*   *   *

Months later, when everyone had all but forgotten he had existed, Our Lord and Saviour returned. Not on a donkey but in Adidas flip-flops. Not to the waving of palm leaves but to welcoming smiles and the silent snaps of smartphone cameras, the tinkle of spare change.

He looked different. His robes were tired and flecked with dirt; his beard looked uneven and patchy, and someone had cut his shoulder-length waves back to an unruly mop that barely reached the nape of his neck. He looked thinner too, frailer somehow. But it was Jesus, alright.

*   *   *

Anyone hoping for the returning Messiah to smash all the parking meters or throw a Molotov cocktail through the window of the local constituency office however, would soon be disappointed, for the Lamb of God had gone Back to Basics. Gone was chat-shit-get-banged Jesus, back was family-friendly Jesus, Jesus for people who wore cardigans and listened to BBC Radio 4; who ordered their Nando's 'mild' and enjoyed watching Vicar of Dibley over a lovely cup of tea. Meekness was back on the menu, boys.

"Love one another," Jesus instructed us. "Be kind."

Saima and I were sharing a spliff on the iron bench across the street, watching dejectedly.

"I miss old Jesus," I said.

Saima missed him even more. "Look how they massacred my boy."

If the people of New Malden shared her heartbreak, they were hiding it well. It only took a day or two for Jesus to fade back into the background, becoming as much of a fixture of the High Street as a post-box or those green metal units (whatever they are). He experimented with signs written on cardboard in marker and at one point wore a crown of thorns (to this day a mystery where he got *any of this shit* from), but to no avail. His primetime slot had ended, he'd had his week topping the charts, the Son of God was old news now. It began to show. He seemed increasingly haggard, weary, his heavenly summons reduced to the dwindling crow of a rooster that knows it's dying. More than once I saw him muttering into a bucket-sized Costa coffee cup. Saima spotted him arguing with a traffic warden and someone on NextDoor claimed that he had been caught shoplifting a bottle of White Ace from Londis.

"Jesus is going off the rails," I wrote to Saima on WhatsApp, forwarding her the post.

And then one day, Jesus got beaten up.

After spending the night in A&E, he reappeared on the High Street one Sunday with a bruised face and his arm held up in a foam sling. A bandage covered a gash near his right temple, and his left eye was swollen and purple. There were spots of blood on his robe, one of the sleeves of which was torn.

No one knew who did it, or why. It had happened on a Friday night apparently, so 'drunken louts' was the general consensus on NextDoor, sprinkled with the usual racist intimations that app inevitably breeds. Saima had texted me the news ("they laid man out"), replete with crying and broken heart emojis.

And that was the beginning of the end of Jesus. The final nail in the crucifix.

For a few days after the incident, the Lamb of God enjoyed a hearty helping of TLC from concerned New Maldeans, who, outraged at what had happened, patted him on the shoulder, slipped him banknotes, or brought him food. But you only had to look at him to see that Jesus was done being Messiah. D-O-N-E.

The last time I saw him was on a drizzly Friday evening around 8pm. I had forgotten my house keys at work and had hopped on a bus to retrieve them. Jesus was sat sheltering from the rain in the entryway of a shuttered betting shop, a can of Brewdog in one hand and a fag in the other. Tough being the Saviour of Mankind. The sling had gone and only a pink scar marked the spot where the bandage was once wrapped. The yellow ghosts of his facial bruising had long since faded away, leaving only a violet penumbra cupping his left eye, which as I passed, looked up into my own. Feeling bad, I rummaged in my pocket, managing to dig out a rumpled fiver that we had been using to snort coke with in the gents' at JD Wetherspoons the night before. I gave it to him.

"Get yourself a drink," I said.

"Cheers pal," he replied, his voice cracking a bit as he enclosed the fiver in his fist.

It was the first and last time I ever spoke to Jesus. The next week, he was gone forever.

* * *

It was one of the last shifts Saima and I had together. After a hairline pass on my retakes I had managed to get a place at Royal Holloway to study English and Film, and she was starting an internship at a media agency near Old Street. Half a year had gone by since the final vision of Our Lord, and he had become just one of those things we reminisced about every now and then as life went on. Omg remember Jesus? What happened to him? What do you think he's up to now?

"Maybe he did go back to heaven after all," I said, when our boy came up in conversation that day. Sitting on the iron bench opposite the Iceland where we had first seen him, we lunched on Pret baguettes, a bit stoned and enjoying the last of September's warmth.

"Fair. Allow this shithole of a planet," Saima concurred through a mouthful of salmon and bread. She had begun wearing glasses a few months ago, the arms tucked under her headscarf.

"I never understood what he wanted," I said.

"What do you mean?"

"Well," I began, swallowing a bite of egg and cress. "He wasn't asking for money or anything."

"People gave him money."

I remembered the gak-powdered fiver I'd given him in the drizzle. "Yeah but he never *asked* for it. So why was he doing it? What did he want?"

"Maybe he didn't *want* anything. Maybe he just wanted us to be better than we are," Saima suggested, waving away a wasp.

"You mean like the real Jesus?"

Saima cocked an eyebrow at me. "How do you know he *wasn't* the real Jesus?"

I laughed. "I supposed I don't," I said with a shrug. "It would be a depressing thought though.

"Why?"

"Well. The real Jesus came back and nobody gave a shit."

Saima scoffed. "It's calm. Nobody gave a shit the first time round."

"Except the Romans."

Stuffing our mouths with the last morsels of bread and scrunching up the wrappings, we got up to go. Saima crushed her empty coke can in her fist and dunked it noisily in the bin as we headed back to work. The new iPhone was out and sold-out, and for the past two days we had been dealing with a relentless onslaught of customers both in-store and on the phone, hectoring us for an iPhone and cursing us when we told them we were out of stock, cursing us again when we told them we weren't certain when the next delivery would be. The madness was upon them. But give it a few months and this newest iPhone would be a relic, a quaint piece of stone-age technology, rumours of the next release already swirling. But this day, the iPhone was all people wanted, and when you looked into their contracting pupils as you told them you didn't have any, you could swear that given the chance, some of them would be ready to spill blood for one.

It was a strange time to be alive.

CJ BOWMAN

Thump Thump

I think my boyfriend has amnesia; he keeps forgetting about our dates. I've been waiting so long in this dull place; I don't know what to do with myself. I take another sip, then hold the negroni against the lamplight, and watch as the red liquid brightens.

I'm so bored I could die in this place.

I glance around the dull room. The standing lamp and its drooping bulb, those gloomy curtains, the sofa with its sagging centre like an awful sunken smile. I sigh, rub my temple, and take another sip.

I suppose I'll do another lap of the room. I run my finger along the yellowing wallpaper, right across the door and over to the wide window. I squint, trying to see outside, but it's not possible through the dirt-coated glass. I can just make out some orangey light, flashing in the dark somewhere. It's probably one of the workmen's lamps.

I try for what feels like the hundredth time to open the window, but the hotel has installed one of those annoying latches that stop people opening wide and throwing themselves out. I give up and sit on the bed – even the springs sound bored to receive me, a creaky yawn.

It wasn't always like this.

When we first stayed in this room, we knew immediately it was for us, our room, there was just something about it. It was different then – the sofa was freshly upholstered with fine, lush velvet, the rug was bright and new, the window always flung open, drawing in a steady stream of light, and the bed springs were always screaming, never yawning. We would stay here all day. We drank so many negronis.

I think my boyfriend has amnesia; he keeps forgetting about our dates. I reach for the negroni but hesitate, there was something in the colour that unsettled me when it flashed that vivid red. I suppose I'll do another lap of the room. I run my finger along the yellowing wallpaper, right across the door and over to the wide window.

I hold my breath for a moment. When I stay still like this, I can hear the workmen outside. Their gravelly movements, the scrape of a shovel, the scrape of your teeth on my neck, sometimes there may be a low murmur, a thud, a thump, thump. A thump, thump like how you'd knock

74

the door sometimes when I'd checked in first, a thump, thump like my heart alone in the dark, waiting.

But this whole neighbourhood has gone downhill. It used to be the fancy part of town. That street, the boulevard, we used to be able to see it through the window, it was all bars and restaurants, pulsing neon, blaring music. Laughter would fly over the trees like startled birds. Yet it always seemed distant somehow. We would watch from the window, sipping negronis, a faraway look in your eyes.

I'm so bored in this place, I feel I could die. I take another sip.

Maybe I'll take a nap; but I'm worried. I don't want to have that dream again. That dream that had me twisting and turning, sweat soaking the sheets. That dream that gave me a headache so bad, it was as if I'd been shot in the head, and when I awoke, I put a finger to my temple, to make sure it was sweat clinging there, not blood.

I look at the clock, is it really that time? Maybe he isn't going to come. I think my boyfriend has amnesia; he keeps forgetting about our dates. Only a swallow remains of the negroni, and it gleams a rich red in the lamplight. I shudder and push it into the shadow. I'll order another, looks like I'm going to be waiting for a while.

I reach for the phone then hesitate. I'll have to talk to the receptionist. The receptionist with her smile, a smile sharp at the edges, and knowing. The one whose dark eyes swell and giggle when she sees me. I hate talking to her and hearing her laughing voice.

I hesitate, but my negroni is sitting all lonely and nearly empty and I feel sad looking at it. So, I pick up the receiver and key zero for reception, and immediately wrench it from my ear.

A howl of static.

It almost deafens me, strangled huffs, hissing. I slam the phone down. What the fuck is wrong with this place?

It wasn't always like this. It was once a great hotel, now they can't even operate their phones. And their gardens are now a noisy construction site. I take a gulp.

Suddenly exhausted, I lay on the bed and pull the blanket around myself. I'll probably get woken up by my boyfriend's thump thump, and he'll be all apologetic for his lateness, and we'll drink a negroni and I awake with a headache so bad it feels like I've been shot in the head, I put a hand to my temple to make sure it's sweat clinging there and not blood.

I sit up, panting, waiting for the tightness in my belly to uncinch. I reach for water but there is only negroni, so I take a gulp to get rid of the taste of dirt. I go to the bathroom and put my lips to the tap, but no water comes out. What is wrong with this place?

Agitated, I take my negroni to the sofa, I need to relax, I don't want you to see me like this. The sofa is lumpy and hard, and one of the buttons is missing. Remember that time I accidentally popped a button on your nice shirt?

I think it happened on this sofa, after some negronis. You froze for a second, your expression hardening, then you burst out laughing, and tore the whole thing off, laughing, buttons flying everywhere, negroni spilling onto your bare chest. You said you'd bought the shirt from one of those expensive shops on the boulevard.

We visited the boulevard together once when the weather was good. I couldn't stop gawping at all those fancy shops, all those fine things. Inside one of the shops you showed me around, animatedly, as it were your home, speaking to the shop assistants so casually, and I felt out of place, childlike, trailing you around.

But even though you were excited, you also seemed edgy, anxious. When I asked you questions your responses were distracted, half put together, as if half your brain was elsewhere.

You were always looking about.

When we turned off onto a side-street and left the boulevard, I noticed your features soften with relief, saw your shoulders sag. You started smiling and gushed about getting back to the hotel so we could have negronis.

I take another sip and start coughing and sputtering. What the hell? Something foul and scratchy on my tongue. I race to the sink and spit out a string of dark gloop, streaks of mud and grit. I try to rinse my mouth but there's no water. I inspect the negroni, but it's clear. Those damn workmen, some of their dirt must've drifted through the window.

I return to the window, the narrow, slit of a window, and peer out. It seems dark out, but it's hard to tell through the film of dirt. I listen for the workmen, I can hear the distant sounds of their digging, their shovels biting into stone, the whoosh of shifting soil.

I think my boyfriend has amnesia; he keeps forgetting about our dates.

I'm so bored. I sigh, rub my temple.

I glance around the room, looking for ways to entertain myself.

The newspaper sits crumpled in the waste basket, its edges poking out like little fingers. Was it you who scrunched it up and threw it in there? I wonder whether I should straighten it out, read through it again, but I hesitate, I don't want to read that story again, about the missing person, that terrible murder, the way they were buried. I felt so uneasy when I read it, the terrible crackle of the page, ink loosened by my sweaty palms.

I decide to do another lap of the room but there's not a lot of space to walk around, so I get back into bed with my negroni, which greets me with a yawn. I guess it doesn't find me so interesting alone, I think it prefers it when we're together. I imagine your face as you thump thump the door and see me in bed with a negroni, waiting for you. I think you'll be smiling. I suppose I should order you a negroni as well, you'll probably forget to order one on your way up. You're so forgetful these days.

Remember when you told me to forget you?

That time I showed up at your house. You hadn't been around for so long and I was feeling kinda blue. I knew where you lived because I'd looked through your wallet once when you were in the shower and memorised the address on your ID card. One late evening, I wandered up your driveway, my eyes bulging, shocked by the grandeur of your place. There are no houses like yours where I come from. When I see the things you have, I wonder why you want to be with someone like me? When you have all this stuff, why do you go to the awful places you go to? The awful places where we first met.

I felt small and ridiculous standing outside your place. I was going to leave but just then you opened the door, holding a binbag, and how awful was your expression when you noticed me, as if someone had just fired a shot at your head.

Your voice was a low growl, grated through clenched teeth. Your fingers on my back felt like clubs, as you turned me towards the driveaway, but then a voice, it came from your house, a sweet, light voice, calling your name with such tenderness. Your eyes ballooned, and your lips formed a silent O and you shoved me into the thicket lining your garden.

Disappear, you'd whispered.

You looked so afraid, so I did exactly what you wanted. I stayed hidden amongst the branches and leaves; my face pressed to the dirt. I was completely still as everything quivered and twitched around me, twigs tickled my face and the slithering of worms and the clicking of beetles and all the while I wondered if your name sounded as tender on my tongue.

When the last light went off in your house, I rose from the bushes, tore through the foliage, and traipsed down your driveway, wiping dirt off my face.

Maybe I should have a shower and freshen up it would be something to do I suppose to pass the time. I look at my nails when did I let them grow so long? Crowned with dirt badly chipped a good scrub is what I need but this room has no bathroom. This hotel has really gone downhill I think my boyfriend has amnesia he keeps forgetting about our dates my heart goes thump thump in the dark waiting. I think there is still a lot of negroni left but it's hard to see in the dark it feels weighty enough in my hand I take a sip. He'll come. He's late sometimes because working in construction is busy he always says. He has meetings and things. And I hope it's that, and not amnesia because it makes me feel awful to imagine his mind becoming white and blank all traces of me disappearing buried beneath absences I couldn't bear for him to forget me like that or maybe you're angry at me for showing up again at your house but I just wanted to see you since you stopped coming to the hotel but as I fret about his amnesiac mind my own becomes dreamy anaemic and I drift and awake with a headache so bad it feels like I've been shot in the head I try to put a hand to my temple to make sure it's sweat clinging there and not blood but I can't move my arms because the walls press against my sides and the ceiling is so close to my head and the air feels hot stale like it isn't moving it's so dark I feel like I'm blind and it's hard to hear anything over the thump thump of my heart but somewhere above me is the workman's shovel digging a thud a thump a thump in the distance I can hear their gravelly movements become quieter quieter and soon it becomes so quiet and I can't even hear my own thump thump only the gentle shifting of the earth the slithering of worms the clicking of beetles

LINNHE HARRISON

Blue

I shut off the gas, take in the A-board and take an extra turn around the trailer to check the locks. I shout 'sorry mate, I'm done for the day' to a slowing Range Rover and receive one horn pip and two fingers.

Fuck's sake.

I head for home with the day's bloated, stinking binbags wobbling and farting in the back of my '00 reg Fiat. A lawnmower with a roof if there ever was one.

Home is filled with identical women. They are engrossed in a ritual that involves powder blue balloons and powder blue bags spewing powder blue tat. Irritability grates away at whatever is left of my energy levels. A loaded version of Chinese whispers follows me as I run the gauntlet of fake tan and terrible eyebrows, through the living room and into the kitchen. My girlfriend is leaning against the chipped laminate worktop. She is wearing grey marl joggers, pink fluffy slippers with unicorn horns and a white crop top that declares the wearer to be 'sorry not sorry' in silver glitter. Behind her there is an A3 poster that says 'but first, coffee' in passive aggressive swirls.

Every room of my tatty one-bed flat has been branded with demands. The bathroom tells us to 'relax' and the bedroom tells us to 'rest'. When I suggested we replace them with 'shit' and 'fuck' I got told to grow up, babes.

'Oh. You're back.'

Her eyes are downcast, taking in her fluffy unicorns. She sounds a bit pissed off. I passed pissed off somewhere on the A66 and am now heading towards rock bottom. 'How long are they going to be here?' I jab a thumb back at the balloons and tittering.

'It's my cousin's *baby* shower.'

That wasn't what I asked.

She brushes past me to re-join her herd, throwing 'I thought we'd talked about your beard, babes' over her shoulder as a verbal hand grenade. It detonates on impact because I'm exhausted, I stink of fried things and I've been flipped off by a vacuous knob driving a Range Rover. I snap at her messy bun.

'You mean *you* talked, while I tried to watch the telly.'

79

The messy bun turns and I notice that she has, at some recent point in time, been crying. I feel I have to say 'what's the matter' even though my current emotional location is a fair few miles away from giving a shit. So I do, and she promptly produces a fresh fountain of tears.

Great.

'Don't you ever think about what I want?'

'Fuck's sake. It's just a beard.'

'It's not just the beard though… is it?' She sniffs and snots and mascara drips down her face. Without makeup, she is beautiful.

I shrug. 'I dunno. I honestly don't know what the fuck you're on about.'

'Oh babes…' She tries on a simpering smile, moves towards me, her hands held out in an imploring gesture. I think she wants to kiss me and I flinch. I don't think this is working.

'I want a *baby*. With you, babes. I can't keep waiting…'

We have been together for eight months. She is 22, I'm 24. Waiting is an option.

I take a step back. 'Jesus, you're not still on about that are you? It's a *person*, not a baby. The baby bit lasts five fucking minutes. We can hardly pay the bills as it is.' The coven of gossipers has fallen quiet. They will be frozen with their heads tilted towards the kitchen, and at least one phone will be capturing the audio for a we-told-you-so What's App group.

Flippancy kicks in as a self-harming defence mechanism.

'And what if it's born with a beard.'

The living room gasps at about the same time a pink slipper-shaped unicorn hits me in the face.

Getting to the apology stage was a long haul. But by the time evening rolled around we had agreed I didn't need to find bedding for the sofa. I take a shower to scour stale fat out of my pores. The beard is still full of soapy suds when the electric meter runs out.

*   *   *

I kick a pizza box under the hedge and squidge the A-board over last night's condoms. Is this a dogging spot now.

Fuck's sake.

I force myself into work mode. My muscles go through the motions. My soul says look at you and your shitty shoebox flat. Your shitty lawnmower car. Your short showers and your shortcomings.

Time develops the consistency of wet cement.

Long hours hold even longer minutes.

On more than one occasion my elbows thudded into the dinted stainless counter as my head sank into my hands. My red oily fingers ploughing furrows through my hair, my body aching with the pointlessness of everything.

Amidst the state of despair, the usual customers come and go. Salesmen – silver tongues wearing well-cut suits driving German cars. Truckdrivers grateful for a calorific bap of grease. At about 2pm I text my girlfriend six hot dog emojis and the sweaty face emoji. As my phone sprinkles me with alternating pink and white love hearts, a rusting LWB Transit heaves itself into the layby.

Its windows are draped in swaying, faded mandala fabric and a comical stove pipe sticks up proudly from the roof. The van stops with an exhausted judder, the driver's door creaks open, a female figure uncurls itself from behind the wheel and heads my way. A lope, rather than a walk. My kneejerk appraisal is Mother Nature on crack, but as she gets nearer, I can sense a warm energy that would perhaps be lacking in a cocaine snorting deity. She's wearing a sheepskin coat that looks twice as old as I am. A deerstalker pinning down curling strands of greying hair. A long skirt and thick boots.

She places a pound coin on the counter. 'Just a tea, luv. Black. Usually make my own but I'm out of gas.'

'Annoying when that happens, eh.' For some reason I need her to know that I too, understand this dilemma, and that we are in some way alike. I pluck a cup from an unbiodegradable stack of empties. Chuck in a teabag, fill it from the water urn.

'May I?' The woman holds up a pack of tobacco and a box of filters. Clinging to her is an aroma similar to the shop in town that sells all that hippy shit.

'Sure.' My 4/5 hygiene rating sticker catches my eye and I add. 'Just maybe not, you know, near the...' I point at the processed meats, spitting and bubbling in their pools of watery fat. '...food.'

She says no worries with no conviction, cradles a rolling paper between her fingers and thumb. Sprinkles in some tobacco. Rolls a neat cigarette with one hand.

I slide the tea over to her. The polystyrene cup is sweating beads of condensation on the inside. The liquid is about as black as my 3am thought processes.

I nod towards the van. 'How do you do that then? I mean, live like that?'

She looks at me.

'You buy a van.' She takes a silver lighter from her pocket, her greeny brown eyes nudged into a teasing glint by the laughter lines below. 'Then you live in it.'

'Yeah, but... how?'

She holds her newly formed rollie between nicotine-stained digits. Her nails look a little dirty. She gestures at my trailer in a manner reminiscent of Captain Jack Sparrow. Or Keith Richards. If they weren't men.

'This yours?' The free-flowing hands reach her face and her lips close on the cigarette.

'Yes.' And then, oversharing like a total idiot. 'My mum helped a bit. I still haven't paid her back.'

She takes the roll-up out of her mouth, and she meets my eye. The gender fluid Keith Sparrow mannerisms start again.

'Sell this. Square up with your mother. Buy a van.'

'It's not worth that much.' It really isn't.

'Buy a cheap van.'

The cigarette goes back between her lips. She angles herself away from the trailer, dipping her head as the lighter clicks. For a brief moment I can see the top of the deer stalker. It has bits of dried grass stuck in the fluffy bits.

I rest my forearms on the counter and lean towards her. 'Then what?' I'm all childlike questions and simplistic body language. I'm Peppa Pig asking Grandpa Pig why the sky is blue.

She frowns, a little, but her eyes still have a grin in them. The glowing roll-up stays in place and it wobbles with her words. The lighter hand continues to live the life of a pirating guitar god(dess).

'Then you live in the van.'

I nod. Impatiently, perhaps. Yes, yes. But.

'But what about money, and all that stuff?'

'You can cook, can't you?'

I glance to my left. An artery clogging tryptic of thin buns, neon margarine and tepid burgers. I look back with a shrug.

'Sure.'

'There you go then.' As if we've just combed through a five-year business plan.

Maybe we just have.

*　*　*

The next few weeks pass like skid marks.

An infinity loop of arguments, silences, make-up sex.

WeBuy(almost)AnyCar.com didn't have much to say about the Fiat, but the catering trailer was gaining traction on eBay. I dove deep into eBay > Campervans & Motorhomes > campervan conversions, resurfacing when required to buy apology flowers from Tesco Express.

The day Buy It Now was clicked by DelBoy66, I emailed PixieUnderTheStars about their '02 reg self-build some work needed. I arranged a date and time for both.

I bought two mandala wall hangings from the hippy shop and hid them in my underpants drawer.

***

The trailer shines full asking price in a fresh coating of raindrops.

I should have done a more thorough stock take. In my desperate enthusiasm I appear to be gifting hundreds of pounds worth of everything included. Industrial quantities of salty sachets, thousands of tomato ketchup slugs. Squeaking polystyrene tentacles surrounding stacks of single use plastic.

So many forks.

DelBoy66 is getting a better deal than I thought he was.

Fuck's sake.

I squirrel a catering pack of teabags and most of the sugars into the boot of the Fiat.

The time is 3.47pm.

We had agreed on 4pm. I was to watch out for a maroon 4x4 pick-up.

My phone vibrates in my hands. A message preview pops up. It's the girlfriend. 'We need to talk, babes.' Alternating blue and pink heart emojis. Four kisses. I shove the phone in my back pocket. Not now. Later. After.

My arse buzzes again, and again. Then it starts ringing. At first, I try to ignore it, but it could be my buyer. Stuck in traffic or landed in the wrong layby. I glance at the notifications. Five text messages, two missed calls and one voicemail, all from the girlfriend. I delete the voicemail because I never listen to them and swipe through the texts.

Hearts, kisses and niceties fade from the messages fairly early on. Call me babes, babes where r u, wtf call me, u bastard, fuck u. I squint at the screen, puzzled and prickly. Is there a way to retrieve deleted voicemails.

The sound of gravel being scrunched by a maroon 4x4 pick-up is quick to divert my attention. Whatever it is, it can wait. I raise a hand in greeting and a shadowy figure proffers me the classic finger-leaves-steering-wheel salutation in return.

The truck growls to a halt, sidelights left to illuminate the diagonal slashes of deteriorating weather, idling engine left to grumble. Del Boy walks towards me through the greying day – a bulky man gripping a bulky envelope, both dotting with rain. My skin tightens, my heart pounds faster and I can feel damp patches spreading under my arms.

Goodbye greasy everything. Hello mandala wall hangings.

My phone burps forth another notification.

Fuck's sake. I open the message.

A photo this time.

Two blue

lines

.

KENNETH HAVEY

Honey

He looks down from the small hill upon which he lives and sees the idiot woman bringing him a dish of honey cakes he doesn't want. He sits, his legs spread apart, his trousers patched at the knees, and his shirt open, in the shade of a twisted carob tree. She climbs the stone steps, carrying the covered dish on the flat of her upturned wrist. She tries not to look at his spread legs, at his open flannel shirt, at the veins which stand out from his forearms. He notices that she is trying not to look, and it amuses him. He reclines in his chair, pushing his feet further apart. One of his arms is over the back of his chair, the other hand resting on the head of his dog. The dog is nursing another litter, which, like all the others, he will drown in the rain barrel. Carefully balancing the honey cakes, she reaches the top of the stone steps. She sees his dark face, wet with sweat, and follows a single drop which runs from his throat to his navel. She goes into the small house behind the twisted carob tree, and clears a space for the dish of honey cakes in the clutter of his kitchen table. As she comes out of the house, she sees that he no longer has an arm over the back of the chair. Instead, he is holding a long stick, which he taps irregularly on the ground. As she passes, on her way to the steps, he calls out: 'You know, I don't like honey cakes. You bring them every day. But I don't like them. Tell your mother, I don't like them.'

But she won't tell her mother any such thing. Her mother will only say again, 'He might be your father, you empty-head.' And then, correcting herself: 'He might be father to half the village, that's what I mean.'

He watches the idiot woman descend the steps. Occasionally, she glances nervously back at him, over her shoulder. He enjoys her nervousness, enjoys the fact that she glances nervously back at him. And then she turns out of sight at the bend in the stony track. There is a towel hanging from the twisted carob tree. He takes it down, and wipes his face and neck. He wipes his hands, each one almost wholly blue-black with scorpion tattoos, scorpions with their tails raised: the work of some cellmate, a cringing little pickpocket – when was it? – twenty-five years ago. He kicks off his shoes, to wipe his feet. His shoes don't have any laces, but it doesn't matter, he thinks, because he doesn't walk anywhere. He sees no point in walking anywhere because people can come to him.

85

'I am my own man,' he thinks. 'Let people come to me, if they want me.'
He is contemptuous of other people, with their hopes and fears and
regrets. 'Hope is a waste of my time. So is fear. And what use is regret? I
have only expectations.' He expects much, always has. Expectations he
has aplenty. And his needs and wants are the same, like an animal. He is
proud to live like an animal. He grasps his dog by the scruff of her neck,
and shakes her. 'What's so wrong with living like an animal, eh?' he says.
'Or dying like one, come to that?'

She walks home along the track, kicking up dust. It used to be a stream,
when her mother was young, but now it is dry and stony, save for the
snowmelt in spring. She stops on the track, and tilts back her head. 'The
sky is so blue, deep blue,' she thinks, 'as blue as the big Cretan sea.' There
are Bee-eaters on the telephone wire, which are more beautiful than
rainbows, she thinks, and sleek as oil. She walks on again, approaching
her home. The yellow grass rustles with lizards. Her mother is inside the
house looking out at her from the kitchen window. She watches her
daughter walking, kicking up dust. She has seen her other three daughters
all married, married and with children of their own. But this simple-
minded one, the eldest: who would have her? Her daughter approaches the
house through the orchard. There are hives between the trees, the paint on
them sun-bleached and peeling. The bees hum deeply. 'The honey is good
this year,' she thinks, 'because the blossom was good.'

He is drowning the puppies in the rain barrel. His dog lies flat to the
ground, her face turned away. One by one the little squeals, no more than
pinpricks of sound, are swallowed up in the dark water. He puts the tiny
bodies in a plastic sack. A breeze circles in the yard, making a chicken
feather dance in a ring. He takes the dish of honey cakes to his chair under
the twisted carob tree. 'I don't like these,' he says to no one. They are each
about the size of a bird's egg. 'She makes them too small,' he thinks.
'Look at that!' And he holds one in the flat of his hand, for no one to see
or remark upon. They are sticky with honey and smell of cinnamon. He
drops one to the ground, for his dog. But she has no appetite. He eats
some, and empties the rest into the plastic sack with the dead pups. He
licks his fingers, and wipes them on his corduroy trousers. 'I've never
liked them,' he thinks.

Her mother asks her about the honey cakes: 'Did he enjoy them?' She
shrugs, simple-mindedly, in reply. The air in the house is so hot and thick,
she feels that it might fall and run in drips. She goes to the basin, pours in
a jug of cold water and washes her face. Her mother tells her to wash her
feet as well. Her mother tosses skinned tomatoes in a bowl. The kitchen
smells of torn basil leaves.

'Tomorrow morning, you can make some more honey cakes,' she says. 'The honey's been good this year.'

Her daughter wordlessly dries her face and feet.

'Oh, and I meant to tell you: your cat is dead,' her mother says. 'I found it, out there. Stupid thing, it had eaten a dead bee. I saw it.' She takes hold of her daughter's arm. 'A dead bee can still sting you. You know that, don't you?' She knocks with a purple knuckle on her daughter's head. 'You know that, don't you? Even dead.' She shakes her by the arm. 'It was coughing and frothing, the cat; I saw it. A horrible end.'

Her daughter's eyes are wet and turned down to the floor.

'But then, I don't suppose you want to hear about all that,' says her mother, fighting the temptation to speak cruelly to her daughter about her cat's miserable death.

* * *

He always begins the day with a whole pot of coffee. He is halfway through when he hears gunshots in the hills, the guns of men hunting rabbits. 'I could just eat some rabbit,' he thinks. 'Rabbit and potatoes— roast potatoes with rosemary.' But all he has in is goat, fatty goat legs hanging from hooks. He will cook the goat and eat it with boiled greens and garlic. He will eat it tonight, straight from his knife, a knife so sharp it can cut leather like dough. He thinks of the idiot woman, and wonders when she'll come today. He thinks of how she walks pigeon-toed. 'But she's not bad-looking,' he says to himself, 'for an idiot. And a woman is a woman, after all.' He reclines in his chair under the twisted carob tree, his legs spread. Looking up, he sees a Bee-eater on the telephone wire. 'A ridiculous bird,' he thinks, 'clownish, like something garbed stupidly for a circus.'

She tries to think of a way to mend the sole of her shoe, which has come loose and hangs off like a tongue. Her mother waits on the honey cake mix to rise; it is nearly ready. The oil is heating in the big steel pan. She calls her daughter to come wet her hands and mould the cakes. 'She always makes them too small,' she thinks, 'like bird's eggs.' Her daughter turns them in the hot oil until they are evenly brown. Then she rolls them in the honey, while her mother fetches the cinnamon. 'He might be your father – the father of many, that is,' she says, 'so make sure the cakes have plenty of honey. It's good honey.'

She remembers him, all those years ago. She'd gone to see him, while he was awaiting trial. She'd walked along beside the stream, and looked up. He'd been sat under the twisted carob tree, with his legs spread, and she'd looked, smiling, at the seam between his spread legs. And she remembers the scent of his eau de cologne, as he'd mouthed at her neck. 'I won't see a woman for a whole year,' he'd said. And so she'd said, 'Okay.' Her husband never knew; they had only been married a few weeks. She'd said nothing because they would probably have killed each other. He didn't have the scorpion tattoos then, she recollects. Those ugly scorpion tattoos, inked on his hands late at night by some common thief. She'd known that his dog then – his long-ago dog – had birthed a litter of six pups, and she'd asked where they were. But he'd said, 'You don't want to worry yourself about them.' And she'd said, 'I could take one off your hands: my husband is looking for a new hunting dog.' 'Then go look in the rain barrel,' he'd laughed. 'Oh,' she'd said, and then put two and two together. 'Ugh, you're a monster,' she'd said, unable, though, to prevent the smile which came against her will. 'I am,' he'd said, content to admit it. She'd put her hand in the honey jar, she recalls, and made him drink it from her fingers, running in light-catching streams into his upturned mouth. 'He must really like honey,' she'd thought. So, thereafter, whenever she'd make honey cakes for him, they were always drenched in it. And she believed, even long after, that he liked her honey cakes, even when the blossom was bad because of spring frosts. And while he was still in prison, quite unknown to him, she'd given birth to a child, a girl, who grew to be an idiot. And he never knew because he and her husband would have destroyed each other. Even after her husband died, she kept her secret and mourned in silent shame. It was better to be quiet, to keep the truth hidden. She sometimes looks at the white scars his teeth made on her shoulders, and remembers his cheap eau de cologne. It's okay to remember, she thinks, but she'll say nothing.

The merciless sun is high over the hills. His dog comes to him panting, comes into the shade of the twisted carob tree. He lays his hand on her head. He looks down and sees the idiot woman coming along the dusty track, carrying another covered dish on her upturned wrist. She shimmers in the heat. The cicadas sing like a clashing of little knives. They sing in waves, waves of little clashing knives. He sits with his legs spread, and as she climbs the steps, she cannot resist glancing up at him. 'The sole of her shoe is hanging off, like a tongue,' he thinks. 'How does her mother let her go out with a broken shoe, like a beggar?' The sole goes ser-lap, ser-lap, ser-lap. 'She usually turns her eyes away, while climbing the stone steps, but today she is looking at me.' It pleases him to see that she's looking at him, albeit simple-mindedly. And when she goes into the house, to make space on the table for the honey cakes, he follows her. Her dress is wet with perspiration and clings to her. 'You're always wearing that scruffy, threadbare dress,' he says. 'That same old dress, printed with sage flowers. Don't you have any others? Perhaps we should get you a new one. And some new shoes.' She makes an appreciative sound, a non-human sound, he thinks, as she smiles at the thought of a new dress and shoes. 'But she's stupid,' he thinks, 'if she believes for a moment that I'd actually put my hand in my pocket for her.' He has brought the stick into the house, the stick with which he tapped irregularly on the ground yesterday. He is leaning against the sink, next to the door, holding the stick. She puts the covered dish of honey cakes in a cleared spot on the table, and makes to leave. But he steps to the side and bars the door. He uses the end of the stick to lift the hem of her dress to her thigh. Her calves are brown, dark brown, but her thighs are almost grey-white. He laughs, and not comprehending, she laughs too. Then he says, 'Come with me. I've something to show you. This way, in here,' and he steers her towards his bedroom. She grins, thinking still of a new dress and shoes, as with the stick outstretched, he prods the door quietly closed. A drop of sweat rolls down her spine, cold as snowmelt.

When she leaves, she is wiping her eyes on the back of her wrists. She tries to remember what he said to her about secrets, tries to comprehend his threats. She glances back at the house, and sees him in the doorway, tucking in his shirt. He puts a quietening finger to his smiling lips. All the way home, she thinks of her mother. Her mother will ask her if he enjoyed the honey cakes. Maybe today she will shake her head, No. 'Perhaps then I won't have to take him honey cakes anymore,' she thinks. 'Perhaps then I won't have to take him honey cakes ever again.'

'What's so bad about living like an animal?' He enjoys the thought, a rare thought. He doesn't care to read, nor does he concern himself with writing; therefore, he has no need, he thinks, of thoughts. 'Thinking is for priests, and schoolteachers, and women.' He slumps down in his chair, his feet crossed, his neck against the chair's back. He looks up into the branches, into the leathery leaves. 'The carob pods are turning brown,' he thinks. 'They were green, a bright green, their spring green. But now they are turning brown.' His chickens scuffle down into the cool dirt in the shade of the brick pile, yellow-eyed, and gasping with pointed tongues. He hears more gunshots, and thinks again of roasted rabbits. And the browning carob pods make him think of chocolate.

She walks in the orchard. She closes her eyes and listens to the bees. The drone sounds as if it's coming from both the sky above her and from somewhere under the earth, making her feet tremble. The bees loop in expansive rings around her. They know her, and are not afraid of her. The light falls in winks and spangles through the leaves. She lifts her face, and the insides of her eyelids are scarlet-red when the light falls on her closed eyes. And the dry grass makes her feet itch. She must have left her shoes at his house, she thinks. She had left hurriedly.

He finds her shoes, one each side of his bed. He laughs to think of her without her shoes, to think of her walking without shoes through the dry and strawy grass.

She remembers how, after it happened, he had held her to him and licked the sweat from her ears, within and without. It made her ears ache, and the flesh of her back crinkle with little spasms. And during it, during what happened, he'd bitten her on each shoulder like an animal. She unbuttons her dress and pulls it from her shoulders, looking at the bites, the near-circles of raspberry-coloured toothmarks. And she recollects that when it, when what happened, was nearly finished, he had made ugly sounds, loud sounds like he was struggling to lift a weight too heavy for him. She vomits between her feet.

As she returns to her mother's house, she finds a dead bee among the stones. The sight of the dead bee makes her sad. She stoops to pick it up, but, as she does so, she remembers her mother knocking on her head with her knuckle and shaking her by the arm. She remembers that even a dead bee can sting, that one dead bee's sting had killed her cat. She wonders what it would be like to be stung in the mouth, in the throat. The thought makes her shut her eyes tight. She doesn't know for certain what it would be like, but she can imagine… But her imagining is interrupted: 'Look, here is an insect on its back with little clockwork legs,' she thinks, putting her fingertip to it. And it clings to her fingertip, as she turns it over; and it creeps and crawls away into the strawy grass.

She wraps the dead bee carefully in a handkerchief.

*   *   *

It is night. Still he sits under the twisted carob tree. The air is quiet and heavy. He watches the moon, which seems so big and round above the hills. 'It is so bright, quivering and bright,' he thinks. 'Almost too bright. And it turns everything in the world blue.' His dog looks blue in the moonlight. 'The hills and the little clouds: they, too, look blue.' He eats the last of the honey cakes. There is honey on his fingers and on his chin. 'She always uses too much honey,' he thinks. 'Although, it's good honey. That must be admitted,' he thinks. 'It's because we had good blossom.' A cockroach emerges with tentative antennae from the brick pile. He stamps on and crushes it, without a thought.

She sits on her bed, still dressed. Something has from time to time been running out of her, cool and sticky; and here it is again. She brings her knees to her mouth, and thinks of what he did. She can hear her sleeping mother breathing noisily in the next room. She looks up, out of the window, at the moon which turns everything in the world blue. Her hands look blue. Her dress printed with sage flowers, hanging from the end of her bed, looks blue. Her mother had asked if he'd enjoyed the honey cakes. She wanted to shake her head, No. But she was afraid to. And now she will have to return there, and take him more honey cakes. She is afraid of him as well. She wishes that she didn't have to take him any more honey cakes. When she finally decides to settle down to sleep, she remembers that she has the dead bee in her pocket, wrapped in a handkerchief. She sets it down carefully on her bedside table. She looks at it, thinking that a dead bee could kill her. She remembers what her mother said about her cat. Again, she squeezes her eyes shut. And an idea comes into her simple head.

When he opens his eyes, it is dawn. He had been dreaming, and he awakes to find himself speaking: '...a woman is a woman, after all.' He laughs at the remembrance of her, of her tiny breasts and her pale-coloured underwear with its frayed elastic. There is a gunshot in the hills. He remembers his brother's rabbits when they lay skinned on the kitchen table with their glossy pink muscles and big round foggy eyes.

Her mother is outside. She can hear her mother slapping at a wall with the flyswat. She goes out to see what her mother is beating at. There are hornets, rust-red and yellow. They come to drink the beads of water on the fat moss around the well. 'We've got to kill them,' her mother says, 'kill them all before they get to our hives.' She knows that hornets will wipe out every hive, so she agrees to help her mother kill them. And then, when the hornets are all dead, she will make the day's honey cakes. The thought of doing so makes her feel afraid. Although, it's not the making of the cakes that scares her. It's the thought of having to take the honey cakes to him – that's the thing. 'But then again,' she thinks, 'today will be different, today will be different.' She rinses the dish under the tap in readiness and sets the cover, folded neatly, beside it. She gently puts a finger to the handkerchief in her pocket.

When he was a young man, he washed every day, and bathed every week. For a woman, he might even wear a splash of eau de cologne. But now that he's approaching middle-age, he has decided that washing and bathing are for weaklings; and it's been a long time since he owned any eau de cologne. 'What's wrong with the smell of sweat?' he says out loud. He pulls on his corduroy trousers, swings on his flannel shirt, and steps into his lace-less shoes. 'Animals don't worry about a little sweat,' he thinks. 'What's so wrong with living like an animal?'

There is a wind picking up. From the south. Soon, he won't be able to see the hills for all the desert dust blown in on the south wind, and he won't be able to sit under his twisted carob tree either, but instead he'll be stuck in the house. It puts him in a bad temper, which he nurses deliberately into a rage. He picks up his stick with the thought of beating his dog. He gets up and looks for his dog, to beat her. And he doesn't believe in restraint, sees no point in it. 'Why contemplate doing something with a full heart,' he thinks, 'but then do it with one only half-full?'

Her mother complains that the south wind will drop half the dust of north Africa on them. 'And I've just washed these windows.' She tuts and shakes her head, as she annoyedly stirs the honey cake mix in a big bowl. Her daughter comes back into the house.

'Are the hornets all dead?'

She doesn't answer but sets the flyswat on the drainer board. From somewhere far off, she hears the wail of a dog in pain.

He looks at himself admiringly in the mirror. He turns his face from side to side, all the while looking at himself with narrowed eyes. He is most handsome from the left, he thinks. He doesn't have even or regular features, though, truth be told. 'But they're strong, manly features,' he thinks; and his face is dark from the sun, which women like. His chest too, where he has his shirt open. And the veins on his arms stand out. 'Yes,' he thinks, 'women like these too: strong and full of blood.' His baptismal cross still hangs below his throat, even though he long ago renounced any thought of God. The crucifix, a sign of a faith he never remembers, is caked with some unidentifiable white scum that he seldom now notices. He takes his seat under the twisted carob tree, his dog hiding, watching him warily from behind the brick pile. Spreading his legs, he waits for her to come again, barefoot through the thornbushes, with her covered dish, like an idiot.

She remembers him saying that he doesn't really care for honey cakes, so she decides to make fewer than usual. 'If he only eats some of them,' she thinks, 'and throws the rest away, he might miss the special one.' She takes the carefully folded handkerchief from her pocket, and lifts out its occupant by a lifeless wing. Then she wets her hands and shapes the cakes, ready for the pan. 'They're quite small,' she thinks, 'no bigger than – oh, I don't know what. They're certainly no more than a mouthful. He'll eat them down quickly.' Her mother is at the kitchen door, cursing the wind: 'My windows, my windows,' she says, waving her fist in the direction of north Africa. Her daughter rolls the cakes in the honey, and sets them on a dish to cool. She sprinkles them with cinnamon, covers the dish with a thin muslin towel, and takes it on the flat of her wrist, gravely, like a sacrament. As she walks through the orchard, she thinks again of her cat and its suffering – dead now and buried in its little grave of dirt. She squeezes her eyes shut at the thought.

He sits in the shelter of the twisted carob tree, scratching his crotch with a veined claw-like hand. He will remain under the tree until the dust turns to clay in his throat, as, eventually, it always does in these storms; only then, he thinks, will he admit defeat and retreat into the house to wait out the days of the south wind. He is squinting through the dust, watching as she climbs the stone steps, carefully balancing the dish on her forearm, her other hand pressing the cover in place against the gale. Her grey-dusted hair is blown to one side, sticking out like clumps of fleece. The sun is hidden, making the day dull and shadowless, and the clouds mount over the hills, heavy with dust, like the trains of ghostly shrouds. The only sound to be heard now is the rush of the wind; the lizards hide quietly in the yellow grass, and even the cicadas are silent in their trees. Her dress again clings to her – not with sweat now, but held against her by the wind. The stone steps are hurting her feet, making her walk unevenly. 'It's unflattering, spoiling the look of her,' he thinks in irritation, and considers reaching for his stick. But then, on second thoughts, he prefers her to be barefoot. It amuses him to think she is hurting her feet to bring him honey cakes he doesn't want. She sets the covered dish down on the kitchen table, her hands trembling. He follows her with his eyes, the buckle of his belt already unfastened. It pleases him that she's trembling, that she's afraid. The air is thick and sour with his sweat, but she raises her face, trying to smell only the sweet cinnamon of the honey cakes. Her mouth is dry. And her feet are bleeding. Her shoes still lie either side of his bed. He eyes the buttons of her old shabby dress printed with sage flowers, that same old threadbare dress which disgusts him. And when he throws off the dish cover, she shuts her eyes tight. He snatches up two honey cakes, dripping in his hand, and tosses one into his mouth. 'A woman is a woman, after all,' he thinks. 'A woman is a woman, yes. And she's not too ugly – not bad-looking at all, for an idiot.'

Western

In Jakarta, my mother is always on the move. Every morning begins with speed walking circuits around our complex (*"At least five miles – for healthy bones!"*). Then she has her church meetings, doctor appointments, acupuncture treatments, family get-togethers, shopping trips and Golden Ladies lunches – weekly gatherings of women who meet to discuss politics, recipes and superstitions. At first, she'd had doubts about this group (*"Too much gossip! So much drama!"*) but that was five years ago and she's continued going ever since.

In Indonesia, my mother speaks to strangers as though she has known them for years. She slings her arm around shopkeepers calling them 'sister' or 'brother' as she bargains them down to their very best price and asks waiters to bring out their favourite dishes on the menu. My mother's phone is always blinking with WhatsApp and WeChat notifications, messages from friends and family asking for her advice; they want to know which salon to go to, which Netflix K-drama to watch next, which Chinese medicines work best for which ailments. They ask her because they know that she knows best.

Here in London, where my mother has come to visit me every summer since I left home, it's as if she knows next to nothing. This is her tenth time visiting me here, and still, she's confused by so much. She doesn't understand how to use the self-service machines in the supermarkets or why some shops won't accept cash or how come she must stand on the right side of the escalator and not directly in the middle of it.

My mother holds Jakarta in one hand. But the shape of London is too awkward for her to wrap her fingers around. Inside my apartment, she perches on the edge of the sofa and squints at her iPad over tortoise-shell glasses that sit low on the shallow bridge of her nose. Pinching and pulling the screen, she studies the tube map, trying to make sense of it all.

"So many lines," she mumbles, "so many colours." She sighs and places the tablet on the coffee table screen down before looking up at me. "Tomorrow, you will take me shopping, Christie?"

My mother can't get to grips with London, but really, she doesn't need to. Though she'd never admit it, she's too nervous to venture outside my apartment alone. She's sure that without me, this city will swallow her whole.

When we go out together, my mother holds onto me, her head bobbing like a buoy by my shoulder. She grips my arm with her chicken-feet fingers and instructs me as I lead her through busy streets and across busy roads. With the pollution and the humidity in Jakarta, it is impossible to explore the city on foot. Here it is all she wants to do. Walk, walk, walk. We go slowly, splitting rushing crowds like boulders in a rapid. I try to ignore the impatient sighs from the commuters overtaking us. My mother simply doesn't hear them.

The walk to Brick Lane is my mother's favourite. With me guiding her, her eyes can wander freely up the modern warehouse conversions, down graffiti-covered alleyways and through window displays showcasing vintage dresses, antique jewellery, iced buns and glazed pastries. When we stop in at shops and cafés, my mother doesn't speak to the shopkeepers or waiters. Here, she flashes them meek smiles from behind my shoulder and whispers in my ear what she'd like me to translate for her. Indonesian words leap from my mother's tongue like crickets. English ones come slow and strained. Oyster sauce trickling through a sieve. My mother isn't sure how to be herself in English. In English, she prefers that I do the talking.

On past visits, I found my mother's dependence on me irritating but this summer, I find myself comforted by it. There have been too many attacks on elderly Asian women – women who look like my mother – for her to be walking around the city alone. These attacks aren't reported on the news. They are broadcast on social media. Desperate, angry appeals accompanied by photographs and videos of frail bodies thrown to the ground, faces bruised and swollen, skin split open like bursting plums, blood settled in the wrinkles. There are other reports too, from all around the world. Of shouting and spitting and beating and stabbing. They say that the 'China Virus' is the cause of the attacks but I know that it's only the excuse. Since moving here for university, I've seen how quickly cultural intrigue can descend into violence. I've learned the difference between "where are you from?" and "where are you from?" I know that it's safer to smile when a stranger says *konichiwa* than to tell them that actually, you are not from Japan. I've learned how to be safe here but my mother has not; she doesn't know. It's my duty to teach her.

As she washes the dishes and arranges them in the dishwasher to dry, I tell her about these recent attacks. She says that I am exaggerating so I present photographs as evidence.

"Look!" I say, thrusting my phone towards her. "See!"

She takes the phone from my hand and pushes her glasses up her nose before taking a closer look.

"Who would do this?" she asks, her eyes widening. "Crazy people," she says, shaking her head. "Crazy, crazy people."

* * *

My one-bedroom apartment sits seven storeys above the streets below. I know that heat rises but I often wonder if sound does too. From up here, we hear lives rush by – dogs barking, partygoers screaming, cars skidding – as if it's all happening right outside the windows. Sometimes, we can even hear the tannoy announcements from the overground station at the end of the road. My mother complains about almost everything in this apartment (and every apartment I have lived in) each time she visits. (*"So small! Too cold! So much dust!"*) But in this one, she at least enjoys the sounds.

"It's the best of both worlds," she says. "You are in the hubbub. But at the same time, you are not."

When my mother uses phrases like *best of both worlds* and *hubbub*, it's as though she is possessed by the ghost of my father. He was born in London and when he died a decade ago, I thought about how I'd be the same age when I left Indonesia as he was when he left London: nineteen. When my father was alive, it had never been a question if I'd move to England for university. I'd study here and then start a high-flying career under the big, bright lights of the capital. This was always the plan. But after the heart attack, everything changed. Leaving Indonesia now meant leaving my mother and although she helped me pack my bags, stowing away packets of instant noodles and boxes of Hello Panda biscuits between my clothes, the resentment lives in her like a splinter, felt only when pressed at the right angles. Tonight, it seems that I've done just that.

"Where have you been, Christie? You didn't reply my messages all day," my mother asks as soon as I walk through the front door. She is sitting at the table, a mountain of our clean underwear in front of her. One by one, she takes the pairs and smooths them out. From the waistband, she rolls the fabric tightly before twisting, turning and folding them into cylinders like spring rolls.

"I was working, mum. I can't just sit around and text you all day."

She glares at me. My work is a sensitive subject. It's been six years since I graduated from university and the prospect of a high-flying career is still only that: a prospect. The way my mother sees it, I've moved seven thousand miles away from her only to flit from one administrative role to the next – the current one being a receptionist at a 24-hour gym.

"It's nine o'clock already. What work they need you to be doing at nine o'clock?"

"Mum, will you just relax?" I say, slinging my bag onto the kitchen counter. "And I told you already, you don't need to fold the underwear like that. I'm just going to shove them into the –"

"Hey! You don't tell me what to do, OK?" she snaps at me. "I'm not a baby, you don't tell me what I do and don't do."

Usually, when my mother is mad, she yells in Indonesian, the hard Rs rolling off her tongue and smacking into the Ds and Ts as they launch from her lips. When she yells at me in English, it's to criticise how 'Western' I am, how 'Western' I continue to become.

There are many things that my mother finds too Western about me, things that she blames on my father, even now that he's dead. Refusing to go to Church – this was Western. Insisting that I was a vegetarian when I was twelve years old – Western. Deciding which chores I wanted to do around the house and demanding pocket money in return – Western. *Too much choice!* she'd say. *Too much freedom!* Choices and freedoms which resulted in my most Western act to date, abandoning my widowed mother.

I know better than to respond when she's in this kind of mood, so I slink off to the bedroom. From behind the door, I hear her clattering in the kitchen, preparing dinner for us. Dinner, which in fact, she started preparing hours ago using the rice cooker that she bought for me on her first visit and which, for the rest of the year, sits collecting dust at the back of a cupboard. It's only when the clattering stops that I decide it's safe to come out again.

* * *

"When will you get a job, huh, Christie? A real job."

We've eaten our dinner without speaking, but now that the bowls are empty, the silence needs to be filled.

"And why don't you go to church anymore? You don't believe in God no more? He asks me where you are, you know? When I go to church, I hear him: *Where is Christie? Where is Christie?*"

I keep my eyes fixed on the bottom of my bowl, using my chopsticks to line up the remaining three grains of rice.

"And how come you are still single? My friends already have grand-children now, you know? You are already twenty-nine and no husband! Not even boyfriend!"

"Actually," I say, raising my head. "I do have a boyfriend." I look at her unblinkingly. "That's why I was back late tonight. I was with my boyfriend."

Although it comes out sounding like a lie, it isn't one. I've been seeing Reuben for nearly four months now.

We met during my first overnight shift. It was almost midnight and the gym was empty. I didn't hear the automatic doors open but I suddenly sensed that I wasn't alone anymore. When I looked up from the computer screen, there he was, standing behind the counter, staring at me. He was tall and broad, with downturned eyes, light brown like butter candies. A curl of his dark hair had fallen to the left of his forehead. Everything about how Reuben looked excited me but mostly it was the way that he looked at me that drew me in. In silence, he stood there scanning my face as if it were an abstract artwork, something that invited some kind of interpretation, some kind of explanation. It made me feel mysterious. It made me feel special.

"Hi," he said finally and I wondered how so much confidence could be packed into a single word. We spoke for a while about the gym's recent refurbishments and then, after scanning himself through the gates, he turned around and asked me for my number. Two days later, we went on our first date.

Reuben suggested a traditional fish and chip shop in north London. When we arrived, a short man in a white apron and matching cap greeted him with a friendly nod. We slid into a red leather booth by the window and Reuben told me that this was his favourite restaurant in the city. I was impressed by the decisiveness of being able to choose a single favourite restaurant and more so that it was something as unremarkable as this. He explained that he wasn't a fan of fine dining and that the best food he'd ever had was during his gap year, eating from street vendors all across Asia. He listed off the countries he'd visited: Korea and Japan, then Thailand, Malaysia and Cambodia.

"I didn't make it to China though," he said, picking up the laminated menu. "Not that I'm sure I'd really want to – no offence or anything."

"Oh, I'm not Chinese," I told him. "I have Chinese ancestry but I'm Indonesian. I was born in Indonesia."

"Right," he said with a slight frown. He paused for a moment. "Well, I was born in Spain. That doesn't make me Spanish."

I didn't know how to respond to this and was relieved when a waiter interrupted us to take our orders. On Reuben's recommendation, I ordered the cod and chips and Reuben got the same as well as a pint of milk.

"It's kind of a ritual I guess," he started explaining before I had a chance to ask. He told me that his father was anaemic so growing up, his family ate red meat almost every night of the week. "And because we can't mix meat and milk, I hardly ever drank milk," he explained. "And I *loved* milk. So whenever we had fish, that was my only chance to have my milk." He smiled at me and sat back in his seat before leaning forward again. "Oh, I'm Jewish by the way," he said.

I realised then that I must have been staring at him the way that he was staring at me the night we'd met, as though he was a mystery, as if he was something that required an explanation.

*   *   *

I'm not sure why exactly I haven't told my mother about Reuben until now but perhaps it's because I wanted to punish her for her constant pestering; I'd probably been wanting to withhold the satisfaction that is now beaming from her face like a floodlight.

"Oh?" she asks, her eyelids snapped back. "You have a boyfriend?" She reaches over the table and pokes me hard in the shoulder. "Christie! Why you didn't tell me?"

"It's still new –"

"Dinner, ok? We go for dinner together with him and his parents while I'm here?"

"His parents? No, mum. Not his parents!" I shake my head and laugh.

"Okay, okay," she says. "Fine. Only him." She smiles and I realise that I've fallen for one of her many negotiation tactics: always asking for more than what she knows she can get. Her eyes light up. "Bring him here. I will cook." She nods to herself as she reaches forward to take my empty bowl.

"All right, all right," I say. I feel a smile creep across my face as I watch my mother saunter to the sink with a bowl in each hand. When the dishes are done, my mother and I sit side by side on the sofa, scrolling on our phones as we listen to a news segment about the health benefits of matcha.

"Huh?!" my mother exclaims suddenly. "This website say you can use ginger instead of galangal." She sucks her teeth and shakes her head. "Rendang is not rendang with no galangal. So stupid." She looks over her glasses at me. "You take me to find galangal here. Then I can make for three of us."

"Yep, okay," I say, reaching for the remote to turn up the volume.

"What's his name?" my mother asks.

"Who?"

"Your boyfriend!"

"Oh. It's Reuben."

"Roo Ben?"

"Reuben."

"Roo Ben," she repeats.

* * *

There are many Asian supermarkets in Hoxton but I only ever go into them after checking if the local Sainsbury's has what I need. I don't need to check to know that it won't stock galangal. I take my mother to the largest one which is a short walk from the apartment. The moment we step through the automatic doors, my mother drops her grip on my arm and walks ahead of me as I shake a metal basket loose from the stack. She glides towards the fluorescent-lit aisles, her shoulders drawn back like a flower opening to the sun. Clutching a hand-scribbled shopping list, she scans the shelves, her lips twitching as she silently reads the labels. I follow behind with the basket in hand, ready to receive the items she will pass back to me.

"See," my mother says when we come to the fresh produce aisle. She holds up two knobbly roots, one in each hand. "Ginger." She holds out the pale yellow one then tosses it back into its crate. "Galangal," she says, lifting the glossy, wood-like root with a satisfied smile. She brings it to her nose and inhales before placing it into the basket. "The website says they are the same, but they're not. See. Different. Very different."

On the way back home, we walk past a charity shop. Halloween is two weeks away and in the front window, there are costumes on display. One mannequin is dressed up as a vampire, another is wearing an American letterman jacket and a werewolf mask, and between them, there is a mannequin wearing a long black wig and a silk red dress with an embroidered golden dragon twisted around the torso.

"Ha!" My mother laughs, bringing her hand up to her mouth. "So funny. They think cheongsam is Halloween costume!" She elbows me in the rib. "Christie, look!"

"I know, mum," I say. "It's not funny. It's racist."

"Huh? Racist?!" She rolls her eyes. "Racist this. Racist that. Tsk, you Westerners. All of you so sensitive."

* * *

"Here, Roo Ben, I serve you," my mother says. She leans over his shoulder and spoons mounds of boiled white rice onto his plate.

Reuben turns his head and thanks her. He is wearing a crisp ironed light blue shirt and smells like citrus. When he walked into the apartment, my mother told him that she liked his perfume.

"It's not called perfume, mum," I said, feeling my eyes roll upwards. "It's cologne."

"Oh," my mother said, taking Reuben's jacket from him. "Sorry, sorry. I like your cologne."

"So, do you like spicy food Roo Ben?" my mother asks, now serving him the rendang.

"Oh yes, love spicy food," he replies, watching the pile of dark beef stew growing on his plate. "Nothing too spicy though."

My mother laughs. "Don't worry, don't worry. I make this rendang not too spicy."

"Stop, mum! That's too much," I say before turning to Reuben for confirmation. "That's too much food right?"

I reach to take the serving spoon from my mother but she swats my hand away.

"He is a growing boy, Christie! So tall. He needs a lot of food. Look at his muscles."

Reuben's cheeks glow as he fidgets with his fork and spoon. I've never seen him like this before, sheepish and unsure.

"Sit down, mum," I say. "I'll serve you."

Finally, my mother surrenders the spoon. She pulls her seat out from under the table and sits down opposite Reuben. I look over at him and see a half-smile pinned on his face. I realise that this is the first time he's been inside my apartment. Our dates always finish back at his place.

"What a good daughter," my mother says. "Christie is a very good daughter."

Reuben smiles at me, watching as I spoon food onto my mother's plate. "Yes," he says. "I can see that."

"You have had rendang before, Roo Ben?"

"Ah, yes I have," he replies. "When I was in Malaysia – I don't know if Christie told you actually, but I spent six months in Asia after I graduated. The food was the best part of it all. Especially the street food," he says, nodding along to his words. "I remember the rendang looking a bit different to this though." He looks down at his plate and nudges the stew with his fork.

Even though he has heard my mother pronounce it twice now (it rhymes with tongue), I notice that Reuben keeps saying 'rendang' in a way that rhymes with 'tang'.

"Oh yeah," I say. "Malaysian rendang is a bit different from the Indonesian kind."

"Not the same," my mother says solemnly. "Try," she says, gesturing to Reuben's plate. "You'll see. Very different."

Reuben looks at my mother and then at me. I realise then, that we are both staring at him. Quickly, I lower my gaze to my plate and load my fork, half with rice, half with rendang, then skewer some green beans on the end.

"Christie tells me you are Jewish," my mother says suddenly. "We do not know any Jewish people. How many Jewish people are living in London?"

"It's not too spicy is it?" I ask quickly, shooting my mother a sharp, disapproving glare. I turn to Reuben who, thankfully, does not seem offended by my mother's ignorant assumption that he would know the answer to her question. My mother blinks at me, confused, but seems to have got the message as she takes her line of questioning in a new direction. She asks Reuben about his work and his family and what it's like to work with his family. It's a relentless interrogation but instead of stopping her, I listen. I watch Reuben get more comfortable as the wine level drops in his glass and he sinks into the sound of his own voice. His answers are long and rambling and I find myself surprised by how little I actually know about him. Of course, I knew that he worked for his father's company and that his long-term plan was to eventually take it over. I hadn't known that his parents were divorced though. Or that he had two sisters. Or that one of them had a baby just two weeks ago.

"Ah, so you are an uncle now," my mother says. "Kau fu!"

"What's that?" Reuben asks.

"It means uncle in Chinese," I say. "Cantonese. Well, maternal uncle, cause it's your sister's baby."

"You said you weren't Chinese!" Reuben says, turning to me and raising his eyebrows.

"Of course we are Chinese," my mother says.

"That's what I said!" Reuben says, looking at her before tilting his chin towards me. "But Christie said she's not."

"*See*," he says, wagging his finger at me. "You *are* Chinese."

My mother laughs in confusion. "Huh? Christie, why you say you are not Chinese?"

"No, I didn't say that," I snap. "I said that even though our ancestors are from China, we are Indonesian. Your grandparents were born in Indonesia, you were born in Indonesia, I was born in Indonesia. We speak Indonesian. I've never even been to China!"

"Oh, yes. Well, we are Indonesian, Roo Ben." My mother turns to face Reuben. "We are Chinese Indonesian," she says. "You see in–"

"It's crazy what's happening in Hong Kong right now," Reuben says suddenly. He reaches for the wine bottle and sets it back down when he sees that it is empty. "Don't you think?" he asks my mother.

102

"Very complicated," my mother says with a sigh and a shrug.

"I don't think it is complicated though," Reuben says, dropping his chin into his hand. "At the end of the day, we're talking about democracy, right? The people's right to choose their government. And China is taking that away from the people of Hong Kong. It's that simple."

My mother shrugs again, shifting in her seat. She looks over at me.

"You like the food?" she asks.

I can see that she wants me to change the topic of conversation.

"It isn't complicated, mum," I say before breaking eye contact with her and looking back at Reuben. "I can't even imagine, like you have choice and freedom of speech your whole life and then, just like that, China comes and takes it from you. It's completely wrong. It's all so backward."

"Exactly," Reuben says nodding emphatically. "Backward is exactly what it is."

My mother stands up from the table. "Everybody finished now?" she asks with a tight smile. She takes away our empty plates without waiting for an answer.

For the rest of the evening, my mother communicates only in shrugs and nods. She serves her homemade pandan cake without introduction, leaving me to explain how it gets its fluorescent green colour and fluffy, chiffon texture. I stumble on the details. I know that I am getting things wrong but my mother doesn't correct me. I'm not sure if she is even listening. She only sits there, scrolling on her phone like a sulking teenager. It's still early when Reuben excuses himself.

"I better set off now," he says. "Big meeting in the morning."

My mother nods from the sofa and says goodbye. "Nice to meet you, Roo Ben," she says, looking up for a moment before returning her attention to her phone.

I walk Reuben to the door and pull it closed behind me. Standing in the hallway, I apologise again for my mother's behaviour. Reuben shakes his head and smiles. I notice his lips and teeth are stained purple.

"It's fine, seriously, it's fine," he says, stroking my arms up and down. "My ex's mother was the same," he tells me. "I know what Asian mums are like."

It's the first time he has ever mentioned his ex to me.

"I'll text you," he says before I can respond. He kisses me on the cheek, skips down the corridor and disappears around the corner towards the elevator doors.

*　*　*

My mother and I clean up in silence. In this small kitchen, we slip and slide past each other, our limbs bending and stretching to avoid touching one another. Usually, my mother keeps even the scraps of any meal but tonight, she scrapes the leftovers into the bin. She is angry. I know I have upset her but I refuse to indulge this attitude. She is being too stubborn, too sensitive.

"Finished," she says, folding a dish towel and placing it on the countertop. "I go to bed now."

My mother and I lie in my bed, back-to-back, the duvet pulled up to our chins. I can feel the silence expanding like a black bubble between us. A part of me wants to say something to pierce it but there is nothing to say so I reach for my phone and begin texting Reuben instead.

"Backward."

"What?" I ask.

"You say China is backward," my mother says.

"I didn't–"

"That phone you are using is made in China. It is backward?" She speaks slowly, as if careful to contain her rage. "All your furniture here also probably Chinese. The furniture is backward too? I am Chinese. You think I am backward?"

I open my mouth to say something but now there is too much to say. Too much because now I know that this isn't about China and it isn't about Hong Kong. It's not about being in Jakarta or moving to London and it's never been about being too Western.

The bubble is in my chest now, filling with black guilt. I inhale deeply, breathing in the scent of my mother's tiger balm swirling around us. I close my eyes and wait for sleep to take me. I wait for the morning. I wait for my mother to forgive me for turning my back on her once again.

Grace

We stop at the store on the way to put the dog down. John wants beer, for after, he says. It's Saturday afternoon, so Kenny and Junior and Mark are standing outside smoking when we pull up and they all nod towards me and go back to their conversation. I stay in the car with the dog, who's lying in the backseat, panting.

When John comes out with the six-pack, he stops to talk to his friends. They all look at the car and Kenny takes his hat off. He shakes his head slowly. I smile at them. Mark, John's best friend since high school, comes to my window.

"Sorry," he says.

"Yeah," I say. "What're you going to do, right?"

"Right," he says. He looks in the backseat. "Good dog," he says.

"Where you doing it?" asks Kenny from the steps by the door. "Pacquette's?"

"Yeah," says John. "We have an appointment." He laughs. "An appointment to kill the dog." He's been calling her "the dog" since we made the appointment yesterday.

Last night, John wanted to have sex. I told him our dog was dying. He said that didn't mean we couldn't have sex, that she wasn't going to die while we were having sex. He told me to stop being melodramatic, that dogs die all the time, that's what they do. It's no big deal.

I took my pillow and a blanket and slept downstairs with the dog.

When we get to the vet, John has already had two beers. He didn't speak for most of the twenty-minute drive and then told me he might start smoking again.

"It'd be nice to be able to hang out with the guys at the store," he said.

"You don't have to smoke to hang out with them," I said. "Don't be an ass," I added.

He turned the radio up.

The parking lot is almost full even though we made the last appointment of the day. I get out of the car and go around to the back seat with the leash in my hand. She wags her tail but doesn't lift her head. I slide my arms beneath her body and pull her to me. She smells like strawberry shampoo. Last night I gave her a bath, lifting her carefully into the tub, running the water until it turned warm. She let me gently lather her up and then rinse the suds off. I talked to her the whole time, listing the birds I'd seen at the feeder, describing the feeling of the grass on my toes, telling her about the first time I saw her. I kept rinsing, running my hands over her ears, her back, her legs, even after the suds were gone and my fingers were wrinkled and cold.

"Get the door for me," I say to John, but he's still in the car. "John," I repeat, "Get the fucking door." But at that moment, Vicki, one of the vet techs comes out to meet us. She closes the car door behind me and puts her hand on my back.

"Hi, baby," she says to the dog, kissing her on the ear. "Come on," she says to me. John is still in the car and I hear him open another beer.

I've done this before, but it's no easier this time, even though I know what to expect. I wonder if I am losing my capacity for loss.

Inside, I sit on the floor, my back against the cool wall, cradling her head in my lap as the drugs do their job. I feel the silkiness of her ear. I rub the spot where her cheek meets her neck. Over and over, I tell her she's a good girl. I can hear a child in the room next door, or maybe it's a dog, a high-pitched sound like a laugh. I want to be able to feel the exact moment when she goes from here to not here. I want there to be a change in the temperature of the room or in the density of the air.

John's not in the car when I come out. I don't even look for him before I drive away.

He's still not home at 9:30. I call his cellphone, but he doesn't pick up. I put my coat on, grab the keys and tell the empty room I'll be right back.

I find him at O'Malley's. Kenny and Junior and Mark are there too. John is in a booth in the corner, his head on the table, asleep or passed out, or somewhere in between.

"He's okay," says Mark, leading me to the bar. He nods at the bartender and then there's a beer in front of me.

"He's an asshole," I say.

"Yes, he is," Mark says.

In the morning, John tells me he thinks he needs a break. He won't look at me. My head hurts from the three beers I had at O'Malley's before the guys carried John to my car, and I can't believe what he just said.

"A break? From what, John?" My brain pounds against my skull and I sit on the couch.

He won't look at me, pours a cup of coffee and goes back into the bedroom.

We got the dog ten years ago, right after we got married. She was John's first dog and so I let him pick her out, let him name her and choose the collar, a red one, because she was black and white and he said it reminded him of that stupid kid's joke. He had so many rules for the dog: no dog on the couch, no dog in the bedroom, no dog on the bed.

At six o'clock I get off the couch to feed the dog. I make it to the mudroom before I remember. John's been gone since noon, when he came out of the bedroom, walked right past me, opened the door, and got into Mark's car. I open a beer, tuck my legs under me on the couch, and stay there until I'm tired enough to sleep.

The next morning I call in sick. I go down to the store to pick up coffee and there's John on the steps with the guys. They're all smoking. I pull back out of the parking lot to get coffee somewhere else.

Four years ago, after my third miscarriage, I told John he could go. We had made it to 20 weeks this time, had found out that it was a girl, that she was a girl. I told him he hadn't signed up for this, that he should go have a family with someone else. I told him that sometimes I felt guilty. I told him I felt so hollow I was afraid to touch anything. I told him I stayed awake some nights so I wouldn't dream, that sometimes days went by without me feeling anything. I told him that sometimes I felt so light I thought I would float away, and that sometimes I felt so heavy I couldn't move. I told him it was too much, that I just couldn't carry it alone anymore. I told him I thought I might break.

We were on the couch, the dog sprawled across our laps.

"It'll be fine," he said, rubbing that spot just behind the dog's right ear. She leaned into his hand, tilting her face. When I didn't say anything else, he said, "It's no big deal. We'll just try again."

Mark calls when I am at the grocery store. I am in the dog food aisle. The bag is already in the cart before I realize it. It's the blue bag with the Yellow Lab on it, running towards the camera, tongue hanging out. I am leaning into the cart to put it back when the phone rings.

Mark tells me John is at his house, that he doesn't know what to do. "Please come," he says.

"Okay," I say, because it seems like the only option.

When I get to Mark's house it's just after four in the afternoon and the sun is high and hot. I roll down the windows in the back, then remember I don't have to. I leave them down anyway.

John is on the couch, his arms around his knees. He doesn't look up. Mark goes into the kitchen and leaves us alone. I sit on the floor with my back against the couch.

She never greeted us at the door when we came home. She'd wait upstairs on her ottoman, the one we bought for us but gave to her after the first night that she claimed it. We laughed about filling the room with ottomans because she loved it so much. John said she must be Turkish, which cracked us up. Our Turkish princess, he called her.

We brought her to a bird sanctuary once because she was a bird dog. "No dogs allowed" the sign clearly said, but there were no other cars around so we grabbed our backpack with a bottle of wine in it and a baguette and ran down the wooden walkway to the overlook. John set out a blanket and we drank wine from the bottle and ripped bread from the baguette and watched our dog chase birds through the reeds.

"We could get arrested," I laughed, one eye on the parking lot.

"If the cops come," he said, "We'll tell them we don't know her."

She slept on our bed every night.

We stay at Mark's house for hours, John on the couch, me on the floor. I am determined not to be the first to speak. Mark has long since left, saying he had errands to do. The house gets darker.

"I keep thinking we have to get home," he says, finally.

I stay quiet. I know how much this matters, this next part, how it will make all the difference.

"It's too much," he says. "I don't think I can do it," he says.

I don't know what specifically he means, that he can't do it. I don't know what the "it" is in that sentence, what's too much, what he can't do, if those are the same. I think about asking him to clarify, to make him name it, to get angry and demand that he talk to me. I think about grabbing him by his shoulders and shaking him and screaming at him to say what he means. I think about pummeling him with my fists until I see him break into pieces in front of me.

"Okay," I say, standing up.

I know I am going to go home now and let myself into the empty house. I will make myself a drink and turn on some music and stay awake until I can't. And tomorrow morning I will go to work and at the end of the day I will come home. And I'll do that again and again. And next month, I will put all of the dog's stuff into a box to bring to the shelter, except her leash, which will stay hanging by the front door until I forget it's there.

ANNA ROUND

That Summer

My father's brother stayed with us, the summer I went blind.

It was 1976. The weather was very hot and I wasn't getting on with my dad. He loved me fiercely but he was a long-distance lorry driver whose whole life was a long gaze into the distance. His nickname was 'Hawkeye', for God's sake.

We lived in England because of my mother, but now she was in Germany with a man she'd met in the pub in Gateshead where she worked; where she'd first met my dad, when he was fresh over from County Kerry. Dad, my brother Frank and I all carried our *missing her* in separate, sealed-up packages, that we dared not unwrap for fear of explosions. We tiptoed round each other in the stuffy house, and got out as much as we could.

And so I hung around with Uncle Matthew.

Matthew was unlike the adult men I knew because you couldn't identify him by his job. My father was a truck driver called Pat, his best mate was a builder called Steve, and my other uncle was a joiner called Gary, but I didn't know how to explain Matthew. He'd been a milkman for a bit, and before that he drove a van for a laundry, and sometimes he served in bars, but none of these felt right. He played in a band, but he wasn't *a drummer called Matthew*, either.

Matthew's girlfriend threw him out of their flat in June and he arrived on our doorstep with a bin bag full of clothes, and his records in a cardboard box. He slept on a mattress in the rickety porch at the back of our house, which Gary was always going to fix and never did.

I was waking very early; it was easier to see in the mornings. I'd slip out of bed, closing my eyes to hoard my remaining sight. The wooden floor and the wall were warm as I felt my way downstairs. Twelve stairs, seven paces along the hallway, three to bring me to the sink where I filled a glass with tepid water. Soon I would be able to do the next things–washing, dressing, brushing my teeth–without seeing. Soon I would have to.

As I drank I watched Matthew stir and stretch through the blurry glass of what had been the back door. He slept with just a sheet to cover him, and by morning his muscular shoulders were exposed and his face was buried in his black curly hair. He looked like a boy, even though he was *old*–he was thirty-six. One day I realised that I would never know how I'd look myself as an adult.

Matthew got up late. I'd spend an hour learning braille, running fingers that felt numb and swollen through the chunky binder they'd given me at the Blind Centre. I learned desperately, helplessness yawning before me like a ravine. (I'd never seen a ravine either, except on television, and now I wouldn't).

Afterwards I crept back up to the bedroom I shared with Frank, although these days he was mostly gone. I reached under his empty bed for his dumbbells and weights, and tied a scarf over my eyes. Then I worked until my arms were on fire and my legs were leaden, and I collapsed face-down on the floorboards before staggering into the bathroom.

When dad was home, he sometimes came in and sat on Frank's bed. The room smelled of his shaving cream, and toast. 'There y'are, son,' he said. 'Did you only just get up? You should get outside, get some air.'

'I was doing braille,' I muttered.

'Your bed's not made.'

'I'll do it now.' I wanted to spend the time with him but I hated how I fumbled through a task that last year I'd have done in minutes. His breath got short and shallow and impatient, as he kept talking to distract himself. Was I going out on my bike? Could I run over to my nan's house, maybe? And where was Frank? Had I seen Frank? When was Frank coming home?

I loved him, and so I pretended I was planning to get on my bike and ride over to see my mother's mother, who worried about us. I didn't ask how he thought I'd manage a two-mile bike ride. I didn't ask where he thought Frank might be.

I struggled to talk to dad, but I sat on the floor outside the bathroom and talked to Matthew, listening to the splash of the water and the buzz of his battery-powered razor. I'd only started to shave the year before and after his bath Matthew helped me learn to do it with my eyes shut, guiding my hand and speaking in a tone so bleached of emotion that I could complete the task without wanting to cry.

Afterwards I said 'Do you want a cup of tea?', because making tea was one of the things I could do easily. Sometimes he said yes, but sometimes he said, 'No, son. Let's get ourselves a proper breakfast.' Matthew had come to England just a year after dad, but his Irish accent was stronger.

Matthew had a battered green van that dad called a disgrace, and we climbed into it and drove to one of the cafes he liked. I remember the smell of bacon and eggs and toast, but most of all I remember the smell of the coffee. No-one else I knew drank coffee made with ground beans, but Matthew wouldn't touch instant. One of our first outings was to his old flat, where he rang the bell to make sure his ex-girlfriend had gone to work and then told me–although I was the worst possible lookout–to keep watch while he ran upstairs and grabbed his electric grinder and stovetop pot.

After breakfast we drove around in the van. We rolled the windows down and turned up the music, and Matt laughed at dirty looks from passers-by. 'Ah, will you look at that aul bugger? He's got a face on him like a cat's arse. Alright, grandad?' I imagined the glares and laughed with him. Often we went to the beach, to walk on sand that burned our feet and swim in the freezing water. Then we lay on the beach, our skin drying salty in the heat while Matthew talked to whoever passed by.

Sometimes it was men, older or his own age, but sometimes it was girls who I knew had slowed to look at Matt. He wore very tight bright red trunks and big dark sunglasses, and his skin was tanned to a deep chestnut. I could see each part of him close-up, but they spotted the whole thing from far off and walked near us on purpose, giggling and shoving one another. 'Good day to you, ladies,' he'd say, and they'd giggle some more and stop to chat. Occasionally I'd hear paper tearing, and then Matthew would say, 'Ah, sure, now where am I going to put this? I've no pockets,' and everyone laughed.

I badly wanted a girlfriend, but I didn't know how to work out if someone was pretty or not. Could I ask her? Was there a pretty kind of voice, that I'd failed to learn about until it was too late? I might have asked Frank, once, but now it was impossible. I couldn't ask dad. I had been about ready to have a girlfriend last summer, and then somehow it didn't happen, because of mum and everything. I was working up to asking Uncle Matthew.

I missed Frank almost as much as I missed mum. Even when he did come home to his bed on the other side of our room, distance fell between us like a steel trap. We'd always been best mates. He was two years older, and I'd been trying to keep up with him since I could walk. I'd learned to ride my bike without stabilisers so we could go on adventures together, stumbled behind him into the waves and swum because the alternative was drowning. When he kissed Natalie Maxwell I'd chatted up her little sister, a thankless task because Sandra was in love with Frank too.

Now we were going in opposite directions, each of us alone. When he was home he spoke in monosyllables and angry grunts, Frank who'd had the gift of the gab since he learned to talk. He and dad sometimes sat in

111

harsh silence across the lounge, not watching *Match of the Day* or *The Generation Game.*

On days when Matthew's band had a concert–a gig, he taught me to say–we didn't go to the sea. Instead I helped him carry his drums, and set them up. To this day I can assemble a drumkit. I loved the pubs and bars and upstairs rooms where the band played because they were almost dark in the daytime. They felt like a leveller. The other guys called me 'roadie', and if I did put stuff in the wrong places or stepped on something by accident, they never complained.

They teased one another mercilessly offstage, but as soon as rehearsals began they were serious. The lead singer was Ben, but Scott, the bass guitarist, was in charge and although he was on the wrong end of the jokes the rest of the time, they did as he said when they started to play. Backstage in the shadows, I floated on noise and the fug of dust, cigarettes, and the plastic smell of the instrument cases.

Usually, Matt dropped me home and then drove back for the gig itself. On nights when I couldn't sleep I heard him come in, creeping upstairs to use the bathroom. Dad, if he was home, almost always called out, 'Christ's sakes, Matthew, will you keep the noise down? There's working folk trying to sleep here,' although if I hadn't been awake already Matthew was far too quiet to wake me. I doubt dad slept all that much in the big, barren double bed.

On the nights when Frank came home, he kicked off his shoes and fell asleep seconds after crashing down in his unwashed sheets. The room filled with sweat and the Pall Malls he smoked, and something else that I couldn't name and I'd never smelled before that summer.

I'd resigned myself to believing that I'd never hear the band perform. I made myself a lonely sandwich and listened to the television until it was time to try and sleep. But one night Matthew said, 'So, Ryan, you wanna hear some real music instead of festering in your room with a bunch of aul' tapes?' And inside my head the world burst into colour.

After their rehearsal we all sat at an outdoor table while Kevin, the keyboard player, went to buy fish and chips. Ben fetched a round of drinks.

'What'll it be for the youngster?' he asked. 'Pint of brown?'

'Coke,' said Matt firmly. 'Jaysus! He's only fifteen.'

I sat between Matthew and Scott, eating as slowly as I could and listening to them talk as I listened to them play; a mass of sound whose detail didn't matter. I'd gladly have traded this for the gig, but at last Scott said, 'OK, lads; no peace for the wicked, which includes you lot. Let's go.'

Glasses snapped down on the table, and leather jackets (which they all wore, despite the heat) creaked. Scott and Matthew were talking softly.

'...and besides, he likes the music,' Matt murmured. 'Sure, it's no harm.'

'He's only fifteen,' said Scott.

'He's got a good head on him. It's just the one night...'

They moved away, and I was about to follow when I heard an incongruous click of high heels on the tarmac. A high pitched laugh, followed by a lower, meaner one.

Scott sucked in air. 'Roddy,' he said, his voice tight.

'Scott.'

I started; I wasn't used to hearing Irish accents, except for dad and Matthew.

'Do Ah not get a hallo, then?' This was a woman, local, and I knew immediately that she was pretty. Gold–her hair, her earrings, her skin–flashed in the sunlight. I couldn't see them, but I thought of candy pink lipstick and blue eyeshadow.

'Hallo,' said Scott. Matt grabbed my elbow. The man, Roddy, made a growling noise.

'Where's the young fella?' he muttered. 'The other one? The *chatty* one?'

I heard Matt open his mouth to speak, but then the woman pushed herself between them. 'Hallo, Irish,' she said. 'I was hoping I'd run into you.'

'We've a gig–where else'd I be?' Matt turned away and dragged me with him, although I didn't want to go.

'And who's this?' Silky clothing rustled and perfume, sweet and flowery with a stab of something darker, stung my throat. She was close enough for her warmth to merge with the evening's. Matt's arm weighed across my shoulder.

'My nephew,' he said.

'I'm Ryan.'

She laughed. 'Well I never. Frankie's little brother?'

'Yeah.'

'Ryan–' There was a warning in Matthew's voice, but the woman laughed again.

'Well, now. Frankie's little brother. I'm going to have to give *you* a big kiss.'

Before anyone could react, blonde and pink and metallic blue swirled, and my lips were caught in a tight circle that tasted like mint and Marlboroughs, and a bit like margarine. My front teeth hit somebody else's tooth. Then it was over as quickly as it happened, and the woman laughed again.

'Fuck's sake,' said Matthew.

'I'm Chrissie,' she said. 'A good friend of Frank's. You be sure and tell him I'll see him later, alright?'

Matt grabbed my shirt and pulled me indoors, hustling me up the stairs. 'Christ,' he said. 'Sorry about that.'

'It's OK.'

Matt gave a harsh laugh. 'Sure it was. From where you were standing. Ah, hell. It's done now. And come here, how'd you like to be backstage tonight, 'stead of out front? Hear the music how the band hear it?'

'I'd… like that,' I said. I wasn't all that bothered, but I knew it was what Matthew wanted. And in fact it was amazing. 'Backstage' was cramped and stuffy, among the heavy drapes that separated the stage from the tiny space full of guitar cases. My metal chair vibrated in time with the bass and my heart sped up as each song reached its climax, Matt drumming wildly until his cymbals crashed into an instant of hollow quiet.

The first set was nearly over when a familiar step sounded on the rickety stairs.

'What the hell are you doing here?' Frank hissed.

'Uncle Matt brought me.'

'He–what? Why–'

'Sshh. They're almost finished.'

'You shouldn't be here.' He scraped another chair across the floor and sat down.

'Your friend came,' I whispered.

'Who?'

'… Chrissie.'

'Chrissie?' Frank swallowed hard. 'Was–was Roddy there?'

'Yeah. He asked about you, too, but–'

'Listen. If they come back again, you don't talk to them. Understood?'

'I didn't say anything.'

I knew he had his back to me; his anger prickled like static. When the last of the applause died down and the band pushed aside the curtains and crowded in around us, Frank jumped to his feet. 'Why's Ryan here?' he yelled at Matt's smell of Cidal soap and suncream.

'He's fine. He's with me. Scott, will you…?'

Cloth rustled as Matt dragged Frank away by his sleeve. I followed, but Scott had his hand on my shoulder.

'Alright, Ryan? What did you think of us, then?'

'It was brilliant,' I said. Suddenly I was furious with Frank for smashing up my night.

'Kid's a critic,' said Ben, and they all laughed.

'Me for the bar, then.' Kevin headed downstairs with the others, but Scott hadn't let go of me.

'Reckon I'll stay here,' he said. 'Get me a pint, yeah, Kev?' Coins rattled. After a moment Kevin said, 'Ah, sure, you lazy git,' and they were gone. Scott said that he had to change a string, and did I want to hear how he tuned the bass?

'Yeah. But…' I bit my lip. 'I'm just going to the toilet.'

Scott hesitated. 'You know where it is?'

I nodded. Waited. No way would he come too. At last he sighed and told me to hurry, and that was all I needed. I slipped down the stairs; outside, even after dusk, the heat wrapped me like a rug. Around the corner Matthew was speaking, low and intense. Frank was there too. He wasn't saying anything, but you don't sleep all your life next to another person without knowing their silence as well as your own.

Matt usually sounded like the beach, like a hot, lazy day with the music cranked up. Now his voice was urgent and angry and scared. Now, he sounded like dad.

'Fuck's sake, Frank,' he demanded. 'How the hell could you be such a bloody fool?'

Frank was all defiance, but it was cracked like a shattered window. 'I've done nothing. Someone's telling him stories. I said nothing–nothing that mattered–'

'Oh my god. It *all* matters, you young eejit. What were you thinking? Shooting your mouth off–'

'It was nothing. *Nothing.* Some guy was talking shite, that's all, and I put him straight. If you could only make Roddy see …'

Matt's voice fell; he'd sunk his head in his hands. 'Oh sweet baby Jesus and the orphans, Frank. I can't *make Roddy see* anything. Least of all that you're more than a cocky little prick with a big gob–'

'Fuck you!' Frank shouted. 'Roddy knows he can trust me. He knows I'd never–'

'Roddy's a fuckin' looper!'

'He's a freedom fighter! He's got off his arse and he's making things happen–'

'He's that alright.' Matthew slammed his fists together.

'And I want make things happen too.' Frank stamped his foot. 'Live my life, not sleep through it. I won't be some sad old loser living in his brother's shed, driving a clapped out van, and playing in a shitty pub band when I'm forty–'

'I'm thirty-six!' yelled Matt. 'And Roddy doesn't give a shit about you unless you're useful to him. Frank, all you can do now is get out an' never say a fucking thing to anyone. I'll help you–'

Gravel crunched under Frank's boots. 'I don't need your help. Anyway, Chrissie'll put in a word for me.'

Matt let out a howl. 'Are you completely stupid? Chrissie–'

'What? You're jealous?'

'In your dreams. Christ, Frank, you're blinder than your brother–'

And then sweat and Pall Malls and the other, new smell were full in my face.

'Ryan!' Frank tried to march me away, so fast that I almost tripped over my own feet. 'You shouldn't be here. He'd no business bringing you.'

'I'm not a baby.' I shoved my elbow hard into his ribs, furious with him and with Matthew. Frank gasped and let go, but I couldn't judge the steps I'd need to get back to the staircase. Frank lunged after me as I ran my arm along the pitted wall.

'You haven't got a clue. God, Ryan! Like I've got time to babysit you, as well as everything else–'

'I didn't ask you to!'

I reached the door and fell inside. Behind me Matthew and Frank were still arguing. Scott clattered downstairs and hustled me back up to the space behind the stage, where they were all smoking in the dark. I started to cough. It was better than crying.

Matt's feet thudded up the last few steps, Frank chasing after him.

'Where the hell have you been?' I knew that Scott wasn't talking just to me. 'We're back on in a minute. Matt, get your arse in gear and get out there. And you two–stay here, OK? I'm not your nursemaid.'

'I'm sorry–' Matthew began, but Scott's bass thrummed from the stage. The curtain swept back and then thudded into place, and Frank and I were both in the dark.

The music was so loud that it filled my head and body, but I could feel my brother a foot or so away; each shuddering sigh, each twitch of his muscles, each time he clenched his teeth and fists. Matt's drumming was febrile, falling ahead of the beat, but he settled down after a couple of songs.

As Ben slid into a slower number, Frank got up and tiptoed down the stairs. Maybe he thought, or hoped, that I wouldn't notice. I was torn between going after him and staying put, and to this day I wish I had made a different choice.

But I didn't. Frank slipped away and I sank into the dark and the music and lost track of time, of him. Once he would have known that I had become someone who sensed, and heard, and felt everything I couldn't see any more, and now he didn't. He hadn't followed me, and now I couldn't follow him, any more. It grew dark outside–it felt dark–and I was in a long, deep tunnel, full of music and promise.

Then Frank's smell, the cigarettes and sweat, was horribly mixed with a metallic stink, and urine, and terror. He was crawling up the stairs, pain in each scrape along the floor. When I bent to reach for him I touched with something sticky on his damp flesh. Somehow I got his arm around my shoulders and dragged him inside. When I tripped over someone's kit bag we fell together onto the dirty lino. Frank moaned, but when I asked him what had happened he couldn't speak. I had no idea what to do, so I held him, my T-shirt wet with his blood and his weak breath on my neck. We lay there until the music stopped.

Then Matt was kneeling beside Frank, swearing. Scott started to shout at him, then stopped and told Kevin to call an ambulance.

'No!' Matthew sprang up and got between Kevin and the stairs. 'Don't do that, for the love of God don't do it.'

'Are you crazy? They've beat the crap out of him, man. He's hurt.'

'And if he goes to hospital the police'll get involved, and...'

'They *should* get involved! Catch the bastards who did this.'

'Scott. I'm begging you.' Matt's voice was ragged. 'It wasn't just... I mean, it was... And they know where he lives, and...' I knew he was pointing at me.

Everything stopped. Then Scott said, 'Bloody hell, Matt.'

We got Frank into the back of the van. Matt wanted me to sit in the front but I wouldn't let go of my brother's hand. 'Are you OK?' I whispered.

He gulped in air, as if each mouthful hurt him. 'Just–get–home.'

'Matt'll be here soon,' I said. 'Or I could drive.'

He managed a spluttering cackle. 'Yeah. Great.'

Outside the band were all arguing. '... a nutter like Roddy!' someone–I thought it was Ben–exclaimed. 'What were you *thinking*, man?'

Finally Matthew slumped into the driver's seat and slammed the door. Scott leaned through the open window.

'Get the kid home,' he said. 'I hope he's OK. But, Matt–we're done. You're a good drummer, but–I'm sorry. No-one decent'll book us if we're involved with...'

He walked away. Matthew yelled after him, 'Ah, fuck yis anyway!' and then we roared out of the car park. Nobody talked much as we drove north. Occasionally Matt asked, 'You alright in there, Frankie?' Frank grunted, and my uncle pushed the van a little faster. In the hot night the smell of blood was foul. Frank's palm was gritty where it had dried, and my shirt began to stick to my chest.

The rest of that night is all pounded into one great mass by the force of the shouting. They shouted–my father, Matt, and even Frank, when he could–until the walls and windows shook and I felt as battered as my brother. Somehow they got Frank into the bath and cleaned his wounds as best they could. Dad told me to fetch Dettol, rags and towels, towels, more towels, most of which I couldn't find in time and he started shouting again. Once Frank was in bed, dad held me at arms length.

'You're a disgrace, Ryan,' he roared. 'Y'look like some pub brawler. Could you not even change your clothes when you came into the house, no? Get out of my sight and get yourself cleaned up, and then I don't want to see hair nor hide of you for a bit.' He shoved me back into the bathroom; my hip banged against the sink and I fought back tears as I stripped off my T-shirt and jeans, and scrubbed my brother's blood off with a nail brush.

Frank was sleeping, with rugged, labouring snores. I couldn't stay in our room. In my clean pyjamas I tiptoed downstairs and curled in a ball behind the sofa. Dad and Matthew were in the kitchen but their voices carried through the thin walls. Even with my hands over my ears I could hear every word.

Frank left the next morning, with dad. He wore Matt's sunglasses, but when I leaned in close to hug him I could see that his face was swollen and bruised, his lip split and a front tooth broken. We didn't say much. 'I'll write,' he muttered but it was probably a joke, and he leaned heavily on our father to limp down the path. The lorry stood outside our house, almost as wide as the street. Frank's fading outline scrambled into the cab.

As luck would have it dad was bound for Holyhead that day. He delivered Frank to the ferry terminal with a one-way ticket in his hand. Our aunt, whom I'd met only twice, collected him at Dún Laoghaire, and a week later he boarded a plane to go and live with our uncle in Toronto. I suppose it was the furthest they could send him from Roddy and all the rest of it, but I more or less lost touch with my brother then; we didn't meet again until we were both past forty, when I couldn't remember what he looked like and now would never know. He sounded the same but tired, as if he'd forever been starting over.

'Put your hand here,' he said. I felt hair and warm skin, and then a dip about the size of my thumb pad. 'That's where they kicked me,' he said.

He'd ended up in a hospital in Canada, but it hadn't been his last beating. I couldn't think of much to say to him. I'd missed him for so long that I'd forgotten who he was.

After Frank had vanished from what was left of my sight, and dad had manoeuvred the lorry onto the main road, Matt came into the lounge. 'Alright, Ryan? How ya' doing?' he asked. I should have been angry about what he'd said, but I couldn't. When it came down to it, he'd included me in whatever it was that bound him, and Frank, and dad.

We sat on the back step and drank tea, and he put his arm around me.

'So,' he said. 'So, your dad's asked me to pack you up a few things and take you round to your nana's. Sure, you'll have a grand time there. She'll spoil you rotten.'

'I don't want to,' I said. 'I'm fine here, with you.'

Matt sighed. 'Ah, no. I have to go. Got a lead on a job, down south, y'know? One of the big London shows, they're auditioning...' His voice trailed off and even though I knew he was lying I loved him more in that moment than ever before. As I listened to him packing, I wondered how I would go to the beach now, or shave, or talk to girls. I thought about how easily I might have found myself sitting next to Frank in my father's cab that morning, and looking constantly, pointlessly, over my shoulder for the next year or more.

'C'mon, Ryan. We haven't much time,' he said. I didn't own a suitcase, so I shoved jeans and T-shirts and underwear into a bin liner, with my braille folder and my school uniform and a couple of sweaters, even though I had forgotten how it felt to be cold.

I suppose I must have returned to the house a few times, but in truth I lived with my grandparents from then on. Dad was there too, when he wasn't working. He was welcomed elaborately, in eternal penance for my mother's desertion. Neither of us was comfortable, though. We spoke little, and were both relieved when I went to college and he returned to Ireland for good.

All that was still to come as I bumped down the stairs with my ungainly luggage and for the last time clambered into Matthew's van, winding down the window and letting in the stuffy heat. He hit the horn twice as we left the street and cranked up the music. 'Ah, there's your woman on the corner shaking her fist at us!' he said. 'Will you look at the puss on her? Alright, grandma!'. Then we were speeding away, warm air rushing past us with the aching memory of time in the scorching sand, or bathed in music and friendship and cigarette smoke.

Outside my grandparents' cottage, Matthew hugged me quickly. 'Look after yoursel', kid,' he said. Before I could answer he was gone. The van

119

sputtered away and I imagined him melting into the distance and the eternal, blazing sun. Without him the summer was over. That night I lay in my orphaned twin bed, listening as the thunder broke, and the rain came at last.

JOHN TAIT

EDC

If you posted a video showing your everyday carry essentials any time between March and August 2023, there is a good chance Mitchell has watched it, has taken notes in his weather-proof pad with his pressurized, bolt-action pen, has added your links to his lists, maybe bought a few things. A keychain prybar. A micro-flashlight. He's probably checked in on your channel since, maybe subscribed. There is a good chance too that, while studying the items laid out on your table or workbench or the hood of your car, Mitchell examined the space beyond, anything he could make out there: the old Harley half-draped in tarp, the movie posters on your mancave walls, maybe the tanned forearms of the woman assisting you. And it's possible, depending on what you showed and what he saw, that Mitchell liked you, or at least thought of you as someone he wished he knew better, who lived closer, maybe even down his street.

If you posted a review of your everyday carry folding knife during those same six months, there's a good chance Mitchell watched this too, wish-listed it, maybe bought one despite the fact he already has a dozen EDC knives, despite Gianna's increased scrutiny with the due date approaching, those sour looks whenever Mitchell returns from the mailbox with any package not from Hanna Andersson or H&M Baby. He may have bought your EDC knife because he liked how it looked in your palm, or maybe because of how you opened it, that wrist flick so fluid he wondered why he couldn't do that, worrying again his hands are getting weak from sitting at a desk all day. He might have bought your knife because of how you shaved paper to test its edge, how you hacked through a broom handle just to show that it could. He might have bought it because of how your video made him imagine some kind of *knife life* – ceaseless slicing and chopping and sawing – which puzzles Mitchell because his own knives only seem to open packages containing other knives.

If you posted a video in spring or summer 2023 demonstrating your EDC multitool, chances are Mitchell watched that too, maybe bought one, unboxed it, unfolded its appendages – all those drivers and plyers and files – and held it like a small metal octopus. He may have bought it even though Gianna has definitely been going through the credit card statements, even though a tool like this makes him think, with a twinge, about his grandfather's toolbox with its corroded latch sitting in their garage, makes him mad again at his dad for letting that particular inheritance rust away. In just one generation, all that knowledge gone. So even that time Mitchell tries to repair the hot water heater himself he ends up needing to call a plumber anyways, lead the guy up into the stifling attic to show him the thing lying there in pieces. Though the plumber doesn't laugh at Mitchell's jokes, doesn't even glance at his special edition, blacked-out multitool in matching leather holster. The shame again, Mitchell retreating to give the plumber space, annoyed at how Gianna keeps fussing over the guy, bringing up donuts and coconut water, barely able to fit her belly through the access.

If Mitchell did subscribe to your EDC channel, there was probably one moment where you earned his trust. Maybe it was the slick way you unfurled your wallet pouch, or when you panned over to show your girlfriend in her tight t-shirt laughing at your jokes. Maybe it was *how* you joked, that mean country wit that reminded him of his grandfather. Maybe it was because you had some great idea he wished he'd had – like his favorite channel, that funny dude who goes to car shows and country music concerts and asks strangers to show off their EDC right there on the spot. Total genius that.

If Mitchell didn't subscribe, it would have been for other reasons. That you seemed fickle, too quick to post your new "must haves" when he'd just begun to check out your old ones. That you puffed or seemed a little too proud of your stuff or yourself. Or it might have been something you said that, while not full-on offensive, was maybe not the sort of thing someone should say out loud. Most likely, though, it was something smaller, maybe the lonely way your voice echoed in your rec room, maybe how you whispered so as to not wake a napping child, maybe that hesitation after you'd shown all you had to show, that self-conscious clearing of the throat, as if you were wondering who you were talking to on the camera's other end and who might be listening there.

If you've ever posted about your EDC sidearm of choice, first understand that Mitchell never imagined owning any kind of firearm before the state laws changed, before the scare with those teens in the theater parking lot, before he watched that interview with the marine vet, who, after showing his EDC knife, his wallet and keychain, flipped his shirt up to reveal the tan holster tucked above his hip. Mitchell's father would have had a fit (Gianna too) if he'd seen Mitchell standing at the glass counter at Century Firearms, staring down at all the Glocks and Sig Sauers. But the gun store owner was friendly, talking about big hands and small ones, about comfort and ease in a way that Mitchell, though this was new to him, got that they were speaking about another kind of comfort, another sort of ease. He understood they were talking about the expression on that marine vet's face, on the faces of those other special forces guys and Navy Seals he's seen interviewed, those select few who know the world's dangers well enough to *truly* prepare. That same expression Mitchell had started to seek in crowds and in old movies, has even practiced some in his car mirror, stuck in traffic on his way home from work.

If you paid any attention in mid-July 2023, you might have noticed Mitchell's own short-lived EDC channel, the lone video he posted, the lighting from the basement fluorescents stark and flat, the phone mic audio not super great. Though he talked Gianna into cohosting, when he asked if she was planning to wear what she had on, she sulked. And then, by the time he brought out his handgun – still a sore point – totally gone back to her HGTV shows upstairs. Mitchell on his own then, setting his phone in its new flexi-tripod, laying his things along a felt strip on the ping pong table: his bug-out bag, his keychain, his knife, his multitool, his gun. Uploading that first video, refreshing and waiting for the first views, the first comments.

"Stop mumbling," writes AkronBob85.

RangerInTraining informs Mitchell that there's a newer version of his EDC knife in M390 steel with titanium scales.

Mitchell knows if he's at all serious about this he will need a better camera, a real microphone, will need to learn to edit and add effects. If he's super serious he will need to post content weekly, even daily, find sponsors, and host giveaways. Probably he will need to script and rehearse, listening again to his voice in that first recording – sounding so tentative, uncertain, too much like someone seeking approval. Whose though? Not AkronBob85 or RangerInTraining, surely. Who gives a shit about them? Though even when Mitchell imagines someone like himself watching, admiring, maybe coveting, that doesn't move him either. Until, in the end, it all gets too confusing, too tiring, makes him watch other videos, even his favorite channels, with restlessness, with resentment. Probably time to pack it in.

You might have noticed in late August 2023, if you were paying attention, that you didn't see Mitchell in the usual places: no comments, no likes, no new subs. Though you couldn't have known this, Mitchell has other things on his mind in August. Urgent things. Sitting beside Gianna in her hospital room, having grim conferences with doctors, reading on his phone about eclampsia and gestational hypertension. The few times he does try and watch his videos, just to distract himself between nurse visits, he can never enjoy them. Even his favorite channel – a classic episode – some shaggy biker at a state fair shyly displaying his belt buckle multitool, his survival canteen full of vodka, then the highlight, his grandfather's perfectly preserved GI-issue Kabar knife. Even this does little for Mitchell, barely able to focus on these treasures, on the banter, the jokes.

And now Gianna's parents are there too, up from Lauderdale, sitting with Mitchell, staring at him, no chance to even glance at his phone. They've never had much use for him, but now they hang on his every word, follow him to the cafeteria and back, even tail him to the restroom and wait outside, until he's surprised to realize they're watching him for how to feel about all this, that they'll respond depending on how he does. And so, he mostly reassures them, paints a rosier picture than any of the doctors have, sees the relief in their faces as they head back to their motel for the night. Then, after they've gone, his own lonely vigil continuing, back in his chair by Gianna's bed, unwatched phone in his palm.

In his stronger moments, Mitchell has told himself he needs to be prepared for the worst, that loss is part of life. He knows this not only from the vets he's watched blinking back tears about fallen buddies in Kandahar, but from his own experiences: two grandparents, a few family pets. In his stronger moments, when he's reassuring Gianna's folks or joking with the Bahamian nurse, he can almost believe that the worst could happen and he could survive somehow, could move on to some new sort of life. In the less proud moments that come after though, sitting by his wife and unborn daughter, one suffering shape under blanket and sheet, that raw panic that rides him, that masters him, those silent pleas, that shameful bargaining, telling God he isn't ready for whatever might be in store. And could they, the three of them, have this reprieve this one time? Just this once? Could Mitchell please have that because he absolutely, truly isn't ready?

If you host any of the EDC channels to which Mitchell formerly subscribed, you might have noticed that some time in early September he un-subbed. It's not anything that you did. It's not the new baby or the scare with Gianna either, though that's certainly part of it. It's not Mitchell's new routine, spread so thin with Gianna still needing lots of rest. If anything, it's just that he's missed too much to ever catch up, such a backlog of reviews and unboxings and comparison tests – so many new mini-tourniquets and luminous night sights and water purification straws. Just too much to track between diaper changes and feedings. And then that interview Mitchell does watch one sleepless night, that ex-DEA guy who, when asked about his *everyday carry*, laughs then shows how to sharpen the plastic Bic pen from his pocket into a dagger on the carpet, demonstrates how to roll a cheap paring knife into a shirttail scabbard. Mitchell excited for just that moment, holding his infant daughter, punchy from lack of sleep, at the idea that maybe *knowledge* is the ultimate everyday carry. A small and bright revelation in the night before the doubt returns. Because surely knowledge isn't enough. Because you need the things too. Because everyone knows that you have to have the things.

And even later, after Mitchell has moved on to new interests, a new life, mostly in love with his baby daughter, things better with Gianna too – this shared purposefulness – he still carries reminders of those past months. A few items sit in his bedside table drawer, a few more in the corner of the garage with the badminton rackets and the drone that never worked. Mitchell still carries his bulky EDC wallet in the glove box of his car, still keeps a bug-out bag in the trunk. Why, he's not sure. Maybe superstition. Maybe because he's better off having them than not. While he doesn't have time these days to dwell on mass shooters or terrorist attacks, there is a chance he might get a nail in his tire while driving to Sonic for Gianna's favorite banana milkshake.

Or maybe he carries them because he still imagines sometimes – though it's embarrassing now, though he's mostly given up on all that – being stopped by some stranger with a camera at a music festival or fourth of July picnic, asked to display what he's carrying right now this moment, to stack everything along a picnic table or the open gate of a pickup. Maybe a few dudes nearby craning their necks to watch. Maybe a woman there too, curious and pretty. Maybe even his daughter, toddling alongside. Mitchell turning to face the camera, hesitating, laughing, finally obliging – neither modest or proud, neither reluctant nor eager, only because he's been asked. Showing each item. Naming each. With affection. With mastery. Laying his things out in their careful geometry while the camera hovers. Showing what he carries each day in readiness, in vigilance. Showing you all of his well-chosen and best-loved things.

ANNABEL WHITE

The Butterfly Boy

He had what she called a starter dick.

'You know,' she said, 'like a good length. But skinny.'

We were sitting in the back of my dad's Fiesta, like every other Wednesday night, the warm weight of a KFC bargain bucket on each of our laps. Our hair was still wet and the air inside the car smelled of chlorine and salt. One by one, Hailey licked the grease off her fingers.

I asked if it hurt.

'A bit,' she said. 'But in a good way. Like it wasn't as bad as I thought it would be.'

She dipped a chip into her pot of ketchup, then placed it on her tongue.

'I don't know,' she said. 'It hurt enough that I know it went in the whole way. Like, enough that I can say I've done it.'

I looked out the window. The night was purple and the lights inside the petrol station were bright. I could see my dad in line. He picked up a bag of Minstrels, placed them on the counter, then gestured out to the darkness, to the backseat where Hailey and I sat, sucking salty flesh from the bone.

'I thought there would be blood. But I guess it wasn't that much bigger than a tampon. You know, one of those super plus ones. At least Toby's wasn't.'

I didn't like the way she said his name, like it was something that belonged to her.

'But obviously I can't speak for all penises.'

'No,' I said as the car door opened and my dad, enveloped in February cold, sat in the driver's seat. 'Obviously not.'

* * *

We were in the water six hours a week. Mondays and Wednesdays and Saturday mornings.

Until last year, Hailey had been the fastest girl on the squad. We're talking fifty-metre freestyle in under thirty seconds, a hundred in just over a minute. She was the kind of swimmer the coach let himself get excited about. A front crawl he saw once a decade.

The rest of us weren't as good but we didn't need to be. We pictured ourselves years down the line, faceless family members and faded living room sofas, screens shining on our smiling faces as Hailey made history in Rio, Tokyo, Paris.

'That girl,' we'd say. 'Hailey McGee. I swam county with her when I was a kid.'

It happened overnight. The Change. Her boobs arrived, then her hips, and you could see it on Coach's face, the total devastation. It was worse for Hailey, of course. The only thing she'd ever been good at, ripped away from her by something as cruel and uncontrollable as biology. I remember it clear as chlorine, the Monday night she walked out in her pink swimsuit, the one she always wore, except it didn't stretch the same way anymore. Above the pool: bright and unforgiving lights. This look on her face I couldn't describe.

We had a meet a week later. Coach still had Hailey down for the one hundred. She was wearing a different swimsuit, a serious charcoal grey, and when the whistle blew, the whole bench held their breath. She led for the first twenty-five, slowed around fifty, and by the end of the race, when her hand slapped the edge of the pool, she'd fallen to third place. Third was fine. Third still qualified for the second heat. But Coach had his head in hands. Hailey ripped off her goggles and stared at the clock. She didn't look confused or disappointed, just like someone being told something they already knew.

We thought she'd quit. Hailey wasn't like the rest of us: in it for the collective success, the routine, the sense of belonging. She swam because she was good at it and it felt good to be the best. We were fourteen that summer and if there was a time to get out it was now. We would lose some of the squad for the usual reasons: girls who didn't like what the sport did to their bodies, girls who dreamed of soft shoulders and delicate arms, girls who wanted their weekends back.

I doubt she would have stayed had it not been for what happened in September.

Outside of swim meets, we never saw the boys' team. They had the pool Tuesdays and Thursdays and Sunday mornings. But in September something went wrong and their Sunday slot was given to Mummy & Me. A different coach might have given them one of our sessions, but the girls' team was winning just as many medals. Regionals were ahead of us, and with or without Hailey, we were going for gold. The decision was final. On Saturday mornings, we would be sharing our pool.

Don't get me wrong, we were ecstatic. All those girls we thought would quit? Suddenly they signed up to swim another season. We passed waterproof mascara around the changing room and checked each other's armpits for stray hairs we might have missed. We laughed louder as we walked to our marks.

And you should have seen Hailey. Back in her element. She could no longer swim the fastest fifty but she could stretch and she could strut. She could do handstands in the shallow end. Hailey understood something we didn't. That to be looked at is to be loved and Coach used to love her. The eyes that watched her now were purer, hungrier. She could feel the warmth of their desire on her smooth and shiny legs.

*　*　*

We gave them nicknames. Like the tall boy with the ears who would chat to us in the carpark. He was the BFG. We called the one with the eyebrows Christian Grey and the guy with the long hair Rapunzel.

It took us a while to clock him. He was quieter than the others, but striking, with white blond ringlets that fell in his face and shiny pool-blue eyes. His arms and legs had the same bright dusting as his head, like someone had sprinkled icing sugar all over him.

It was a Saturday in October. We were doing time trials and Coach had us out of the water. It was important, he said, to recreate the atmosphere of an actual heat. He wanted bodies on the benches, noise in the air.

We alternated, girls then boys, freestyle, backstroke, then butterfly. We sat on the bench, sometimes watching the boys but more often watching ourselves. The spread of our flesh on the plastic. Our stomachs and our thighs. We stared at our reflections in the window. The shape of our scalps in those shiny red caps. We weren't watching when they started the butterfly. We didn't look up as he dove into the water, nor did we see his body ripple under the surface like it was something he was born to do.

Zoe said she saw him first, but Lauren claimed it was her. However it happened, one by one we fell silent. I was next to Nia at the end of the bench, picking at my nails. I heard the word *fuck* as it slipped from her lips.

What we could agree on: the speed, the strength, the shoulders that stretched out the water, like something sculpted from clay. Coach pacing the deep end, his eyes moving from the boy in the pool to the clock on the wall. The slap of his feet against the floor.

In hindsight, his backstroke was nothing special and his breaststroke was kind of sloppy, but we didn't care. From that day on, he was our Butterfly Boy.

We'd gather in the changing room after practice, delighting in the memory of his arms, how they tore through the water. The shape of his mouth as he came up for breath. That perfect circular O. In the damp dark,

128

we'd sit on benches, lean against lockers, wring water from our limp ponytails. We'd dream aloud about the tickle of fuzz under his arms, his small pink nipples and what it might be like to suck on them. We avoided speaking to him whenever we could. We feared the pressure of saying the right words, contorting our faces into acceptable expressions. We needed the safety of distance, the freedom to love him from afar.

Together we collected information. Megan saw him at the big Tesco by the stadium, which is how we learned he lived south of town.

'He was holding a can of Sure deodorant,' she told us. 'And a packet of Doritos Chilli Heatwave. And when he looked at me, he nodded. He actually freaking nodded.'

We groaned with envy.

Nia saw him at the bus stop wearing a blazer and tie, which is how we learned he was a private school boy, but then Sofia saw him in Fajita City, black trousers and pink polo, clearing plates and wiping tables. We delighted in this detail. He must be poor! A scholarship boy! Clever, well-mannered, unaccustomed to the presence of girls. We'd show him the ways of the world.

I saw him once. A grey Sunday in November. Service in session, hymns rumbling out of the church. We'd gone to visit my grandma, to replace the flowers. The grass was frosted over and it crunched under my feet. He had his back to me, but I knew from the shape of his shoulders. He stood with his mother, and a smaller girl, maybe nine or ten, in a pink puffer jacket. All three had the same soft curls.

The woman and the girl walked towards the car, but Butterfly Boy stayed standing. The gravestone was nothing like the faded cement of my grandmother's. Instead, shiny marble with gold carved writing. His lips were moving and I watched him wipe his eyes.

* * *

'It's funny because his pubes are, like, bright blonde too. I've never seen anything like it.'

It was Saturday, nine am. Hailey stood in the middle of the changing room, pulling a paddle brush through her hair. Long dark strands floated to the floor.

'I honestly wish I could have taken a picture for you guys. You would not have believed it.'

We sat stony-faced on the benches. Nia spoke first.

'I don't understand,' she said. 'How did this happen?'

129

If Hailey thought we'd be excited for her, she was wrong. There was a sadness in the air that day. She'd taken something we shared and she'd broken it.

'So you know how my cousin's like three years above. Well, it was her eighteenth last Saturday so she booked this massive table at Fajita City. And obviously Toby works there, and we were sat in his section and he kept coming over to our table, all like, "What can I get you guys?" and it was so fucking adorable and mortifying all at once. We were ordering all these drinks and no one was checking ID, I guess because half the table was legal, and yeah we literally just stayed at Fajita City till like 11pm. So it was us and Butterfly – sorry, Toby – and a couple of other waiters behind the bar. And my cousin's got this friend called Dylan and he's got this place they all go called the Den. It's basically this shed at the end of his garden but it's got like a TV and sofas and stuff. So he was all like, "Let's go back to the Den, let's go back to the Den," and Toby was just wiping the tables, and I was like, "Fuck it, I'm gonna invite him." Like yolo, you know. Anyway a group of us went back to the Den, and we were just like sat on these sofas, drinking and stuff, and I could feel Toby looking at me, so I was like, "Dyl, where's your toilet?" even though I knew it was in the house, and he was like, "Go inside, then take a left after the kitchen, blah, blah, blah," and so I got to the bathroom and I didn't even lock the door, because I kind of just knew. I was like, "Right, Hailey. Count to ten and if he's not here, just go back to the party." I didn't even need to pee. I just stood there, like, looking in the mirror, and I got to seven and there was a knock on the door.'

'Sorry. What the fuck?' This was Megan talking. The one he nodded at in big Tesco. 'You had sex with Butterfly Boy in a toilet?'

A thump on the door. Coach's voice, loud and clear: 'Get a move on, girls.'

We walked out the changing room single file. Butterfly Boy was already in the water, flapping around on his back. It was like he wanted us to watch him, to stare at the bulge of his speedos. I pictured his dick curled inside them, that bed of bright blonde pubes.

* * *

We never saw them speak. Not before swimming, not after, not standing in the car park, waiting for my dad or hers.

'It's chill,' Hailey said when I asked her about it. 'It was a one time thing. It's not like we're going out now.'

* * *

Then it was March, a Wednesday night. Regionals were a week away and Hailey and I were leaving the pool. My dad was waiting in his car and we were walking towards him, hungry and hopeful for burgers. Coach pulled me aside by the automatic doors.

'Alice.'

You'd have thought he'd said Hailey's name, the way her head flicked around, her eyes wide and waiting.

'Great job today.'

'Thanks, Coach.'

He breathed on his hands and rubbed them together. His fingers were thick and sausage-like.

'How would you feel about doing the medley next week?'

I gripped the straps of my backpack. 'Um, yeah. Sure. That would be amazing.'

A smile spread across his face. 'That butterfly of yours is really coming along. You're giving Toby a run for his money.'

In the car, my dad had the heating on blast. Hailey took the front seat.

'Good session?'

'Great,' said Hailey. I couldn't see her face. 'Ali's swimming the medley at regionals.'

'Alice, that's brilliant.'

'Yeah, it's no big deal,' I said.

We drove out of the car park in silence. I felt like I had something to apologise for, but I wasn't sure what it was. We pulled up outside McDonald's and my dad passed me his card.

'Whatever you want,' he smiled. 'You've got a medley to load up for.'

Hailey ordered nuggets and a strawberry milkshake. I got a Big Mac and chips. While we waited, she took a circular tin of Vaseline out of her pocket. I watched as she smeared clear grease over her lips.

'Toby looked good on Saturday,' she said.

'What?'

'Toby. Butterfly Boy. He looked hot.'

'Oh,' I said. 'Yeah.'

She tilted her head, looked at me.

'You like him too, don't you?'

'I guess. We all do.'

'No, but you really like him.'

Our number was called. We picked up the warm brown bags and walked towards the car. It was dark outside. A streetlight flickered, off then on.

'I might do it again.'

'Do what again?'

'Fuck him.'

I wasn't sure what I was supposed to say.

'Or you could,' she said.

'I'm obviously not going to do that.'

My dad looked up from the driver's seat. Waved at us.

'You're the right choice for the medley,' she said, her voice quieter now. 'Like I almost felt proud watching you swim today.'

'Oh. Thanks.'

She sighed. 'It actually made me miss having no tits.'

* * *

We drove separately to regionals. I was sitting in the stands, tracksuit over my swimsuit, my parents either side of me. My mum was the one to notice them.

'Oh look,' she said. 'There's Joanne. And Hailey.'

Hailey stood behind her mother, her hair in two plaits that ran down the length of her back. She looked around the pool blankly and took a bite of her breakfast bar.

The races were split into categories: distance, age, gender. There were heats and there were finals and there were ceremonies where tired teenagers had medals dropped around their necks. We broke for lunch and we did it all again.

Before his race, Toby stood at the deep end, his chest swelling as he took short, fast breaths. He swung his arms in circles and stared out the water. We watched from the benches as he powered through the pool. Hand in hand, screaming our throats raw, we forgot what Hailey had done to us, what she'd taken. For a split-second, he was our swimmer and our teammate. He was our Butterfly Boy.

I rose from the stands for the individual medley. The final race of the day. I took my mark and stared at the flat expanse of turquoise before me. The whistle blew and we went.

Hailey used to say she knew when she was winning. If a swimmer six lanes down was about to take her, she could feel it in the water. I was never sure if this was true or something she just liked to say. Another reason she was different to us, better than us. Hailey, the shark, sensing her prey from hundreds of miles away.

But I felt it in the moment I flipped onto my back. Not in my arms or legs, but deeper inside me. The possibility that the race might be mine.

Length three was breaststroke. Focused breathing, flexed toes, dipping into the crash of the water, back into the screams of the crowd.

The key, Coach always told us, during a race is to think of everything you can except swimming. While you're pumping your legs as fast as they can go, take your mind out of the pool. Think of a place, he'd say. And go there.

My dad's car. The backseat with Hailey. The chicken and the chlorine and the salt. Coach. His clean white trainers. Their smack on the tiles. I moved into front crawl and it was Hailey again. Butterfly Boy. Their bodies pushed against the back of a bathroom door. Her voice in my head.

You like him too, don't you?

I powered through the final length and when my hand hit the edge of the pool, I could feel it. The roar. I pulled off my goggles and took it all in. Coach's fist in the air. That face my dad makes when he's trying not to cry. My teammates, screaming.

Hailey sat next to her mother, three rows from the front. No smile, no cheer. Just a slow, obligatory clap.

* * *

The house sat at the top of a hill, behind a gate you had to buzz for. It was big and modern, a cream-painted block with floor-to-ceiling windows. I walked fast up the pavement. The night was black and the moon was a thin white curl. A fingernail clipping in the sky.

There was no real reason for me to lie. If I'd told my dad where I was going, he would have dropped me. But there was something about the secrecy I was drawn to. Placing first in the medley had brought us to the top of the leaderboard and it was like a switch had gone off inside me. Tonight I wore eyeshadow and lip gloss. I walked through the dark in a cloud of Impulse Serenity and I felt like I existed.

Lauren's jeans were covered in tiny diamantés. Her black top wrapped around her in a web of string.

'She's here,' she said, standing on her porch. 'The champion.'

Her eyes were circled in black pencil and her hair was pulled into a long blonde ponytail. It was the first time I'd seen her outside of swimming.

'You look amazing.'

'Oh my god,' she said. 'So do you.'

Inside the house, music seemed to emanate out of the walls. Soft and slow, the kind of songs you hear in movies. I asked who else was here.

'Megan and Nia and Zoe so far. Jess and Sofia are almost here. Then out of the boys, just Miles and Kieran and Toby.'

We didn't use the nicknames when they were in earshot.

'Oh, yeah,' Lauren said. 'And Hailey's coming later.'

She opened a fridge to reveal neat rows of beer.

'What do you want to drink? We've got wine and beer and cider. Megan brought some vodka, but I feel like we stay off the hard stuff. At least till a bit later.'

'Sure. What are you having?'

She nodded to the beer on the table. 'I'm on the Heineken.'

'Okay, yeah. I'll have the same.'

* * *

We were outside when Hailey arrived. It was late and a cigarette was making its way around the circle. When it came to me, I brought the damp tip to my lips and breathed in.

'Well, well, well. Who would have thought it? Sweet little Alice smoking her first fag.'

The house connected to the garden through sliding glass doors. Hailey was a silhouette against the bright lights.

The girls stood up and hugged her. I'd held the smoke for too long and I coughed as it scratched its way out of me. The cigarette was small, almost pathetic to look at, but it burned.

Butterfly Boy was on my left and I passed it to him. The others had dispersed inside but the two of us stayed seated. Through the glass I could see Hailey leaning against the kitchen island. She was showing Zoe something on her phone. Her eyes flicked up in our direction, then back to her screen. I was glad to be out here, alone with Butterfly Boy. I was glad to be making her hurt.

'I don't use this word much,' he said. His eyes were closed and he sucked on the stub of the cigarette. 'But your friend's kind of a bitch.'

'Hailey?'

He nodded. Inside I heard laughter. Out in the garden the only noise was the whoosh of wind through the trees. I opened my can of beer and watched white foam spit up through the hole. I was aware of him looking at me, waiting for me to say something. I took a sip.

'She's complicated. And she's jealous. She used to be the fastest and she's not anymore and I guess that stings.' I felt something small and hard in my throat. 'But you're probably the last person she'd want me to have this conversation with.'

134

'Why's that?'

'Because of what happened with you guys.'

A thin V formed between his brows. He opened his mouth like he was going to say something but stopped. A shadow fell over us and we looked up to see Hailey leaning against the door.

'Hope I'm not interrupting anything.'

The light was behind her so at first I couldn't see her face. I leaned in closer to Butterfly Boy.

'No,' I said. 'We were just chatting.'

She looked from me to him, then back again. It took me a moment to recognise the expression on her face for what it was.

Fear.

* * *

It was a stupid party, so we played stupid games. Truth or dare, spin the bottle, seven minutes in heaven. There was a cupboard off the living room with dusty board games and broken toys and just enough floor space for two. The rules were simple. You spun the bottle and you went inside.

The light was low and we sat on the living room floor, our backs against the sofas. Hailey and Zoe came out giggling.

'We kissed,' Hailey announced to the room. 'For like the whole seven minutes.'

She stumbled back to her place on the floor and I wondered if she was really that drunk or just pretending.

* * *

A memory that came to me as we watched the bottle spin:

Year Four. Rebecca Roberts got a poodle and her mum brought it to pick-up. We swarmed the thing. Stroking it and kissing it and speaking in these stupid baby voices. Hailey made a point of standing back and watching us.

'I thought you loved dogs,' I said to her.

'I did.' Her voice was slow and sour. 'Until mine died.'

Her mum had bought her a puppy, she told us, just a few weeks ago. They called it Snowy and on the third day they had it Snowy had been hit by a car. We stood around her in a circle at the gates.

'I didn't tell anyone,' she said, wiping her eyes with the sleeves of her school jumper.

Now in the living room the bottle started to slow. The realisation came to me as the lips of the smeared Corona stopped on Toby. Snowy had never existed. The whole thing had been a lie.

*   *   *

I might have been scared. If I hadn't won the medley. If I hadn't decided I wasn't her friend. If I hadn't believed she was a liar. I might have been nervous standing across from him, a single bulb hanging from the cupboard ceiling, showering us in harsh white light.

It was bumpy, the way he kissed me. His lips were wet and slug-like. His teeth knocked mine, his tongue moving in fast, wide circles. I could stop. I knew whenever I wanted I could stop, but right before I opened my eyes I'd see her, standing in the changing room, brushing her long dark hair. I'd hear the giggle in her voice. *His pubes are, like, bright blonde too.*

I hadn't touched one before. I'd seen pictures and knew essentially the motion I needed to make. I vaguely remembered a list of do's and don'ts I'd read online. Something about the balls? Keeping a steady rhythm? His mouth was on my ear now, hot and breathy. I could hear the murmur of voices outside.

When he came it was white and shiny. The same colour and consistency as the shampoo in the dispensers at the pool. He smiled, almost shyly, then looked around and settled on a toy rabbit on the bottom shelf. It was tired and grey, chewed on by a child or maybe a dog. He passed it to me and I used its thin floppy ears to wipe each of my fingers.

'Sorry, bunny,' I whispered. Butterfly Boy laughed.

He brought his dick out his pants and wiped himself on the grey matted fur. It felt intimate somehow, watching him do this, more so than the moments preceding it. His hair down there was brown and fuzzy. The colour of dirty dishwater.

*   *   *

Hailey sat on Lauren's brother's bed, cleaning her face with a Simple wipe. She smiled as I came in, the kind of lips-together smile you give someone you don't know very well. The room was small but neat. Blue checked duvet, a bedside light shaped like a rocket, the lampshade a dark and starry sky. A sheetless mattress had been pulled out from under the bed, a sleeping bag thrown across it. She offered me the wipes and I took one.

136

Hailey hadn't been in the living room when I came out the cupboard. We'd played another round before Lauren called it a night, before boy-girl pairings slunk off upstairs and bodies tried to find beds wherever they could.

'It's kind of gross,' she said, holding the wipe in front of her. It was streaked with pink and beige and black. 'The shit we put on our faces.'

'Yeah,' I said.

I passed her the wipes and she put them in her backpack.

'Nia and Kieran were all over each other,' she said. 'I wouldn't be surprised if they do it tonight. She's so desperate to lose it.'

She balanced her phone against the bedside light and opened her camera app. Pouting into the screen, she rubbed moisturiser into her cheeks.

'Did you actually see him?' I asked, my voice as gentle as I could make it. 'That night in Fajita City. Like, was he even there?'

I was ready for her to brush me off or laugh in my face, but she looked at me surprised. When she spoke her voice was barely a whisper.

'Are you going to tell?' she asked.

I shook my head and we looked at each other. The truth would come out and I knew that she knew that. Without her makeup she looked younger. I thought of the day we met. It was halfway through the school year and Hailey, age eight, stood at the door of the classroom. She'd clung to her mum with both arms.

'No,' I said. 'I don't think so.'

She chose then to tell me. She wasn't swimming another season. It was taking up too much time, she explained. Her mum wanted her to focus on exams.

'Oh,' I said.

'Do you want the bed?' she asked.

'It's fine,' I told her. 'You were here first.'

We lay in silence for a moment and my mind spun with the words I wanted to say. I wondered if I'd miss her or whether I should at least say that I would. Lauren's brother had pushed plastic stars onto his ceiling and even with the rocket lamp still on, they emitted a watery yellow glow. I thought maybe I'd tell her I forgave her, that I forgave her even though she hadn't said sorry, but then I heard her breathe in and out.

She turned off the light.

ANGELA WIPPERMAN

They Cling Tightly

When Lewis was ten, and I was twelve, we went on a family holiday to Ireland. We stayed in a cottage near the beach in Cork, and I took Lewis hunting for mussels that our dad would later steam until their mouths opened in wet sighs.

I started at it, showing him how to twist, rather than pull the shiny, black shells. He followed behind, climbing tentatively over the rocks that were slick with seaweed. The sky was grey, and the air full of drizzle. It smelled of sea salt, and peat. At some point I turned back to check how he was doing, and saw that his bucket was empty.

"What have you been doing? Why haven't you got any?"

"I can't."

"But I showed you. Look, you twist it. If you just pull, they won't come off."

"I know. I know how. I don't want to."

"Why?"

He winced, and I knew what it was.

"They're not animals, Lewis," I said. "They're not animals like dogs and cats. They're not even fish. They're basically plants. They don't know anything."

"But if they didn't want to live, why would they hold on?"

"It's just how they're made. It doesn't mean anything."

But he wouldn't do it. I took his bucket, and filled them both.

* * *

I thought I might become a psychiatrist. In my personal statement, I wrote:

I hope to specialise in psychiatry, owing to my family history with mental illness. I would love to be able to effect change in a field that I have been so personally affected by.

Then I took a psychiatry module in third year. We had a small group seminar, during which the tutor talked us through the biopsychosocial while simultaneously working on a falafel wrap. After one large bite, a globe of garlic mayonnaise caught and hung in his moustache.

"Don't think as a psychiatrist you can fix anything," he said. "If you want to fix things, become an orthopaedic surgeon, or a cardiologist. Psychiatry is a specialty of management, not cure."

* * *

When they got into fights, it was like watching two meteorological events collide. A thunderstorm meeting a whirlwind. They spoke different languages. My dad yelled and slammed tables; Lewis cried. Mum and I watched from the relative safety of other rooms, or the top of stairs.

"Shall I go down?" she'd say. "I'll go down."

But she never did, not until the inevitable settling of the eerie quiet. Then she'd swoop into the kitchen or the living room or the garden, or wherever their bodies had ended up after being tossed about by rage and misunderstanding, and put her arms around the body of her son which had become a head taller than her own. And in her soft arms and her gentle shushing, there was nowhere for the fight to go.

Then there was the time Lewis said, quietly, in between sobs, "Fuck you, you bastard", and my father hit him.

* * *

There was some worrying streak that ran through my family. An undercurrent, a disturbance. My mother's father, my father's sister, my mother's cousin. There were gaps in the family tree, lines that ended in mid-air. They would say, '*she was a bit funny, Granny Iris*', '*Arthur was touched, as they used to say*', '*your Aunt struggled with life*'.

* * *

I decided I would become a cardiologist. You can open a body and look at a heart. Four chambers, four valves. Like a machine it has instructions and if it's not working, all you have to do is go through it piece by piece and check each part for faults. A brain is much harder to fathom. It can only be segmented to a degree. You can watch the sped-up scans from the fMRI. The dancing shadows that show us, in their rawest form, love, sex, hate, sadness. But those dancing shadows are a language we don't yet fully understand. They transcend our small biology.

* * *

When he dropped out of uni, we didn't tell our parents. Lewis came to stay with me in the flat I shared in Wimbledon. It was a shock to see him so thin. He slept in my bed, and it reminded me of the way we'd shared on those holidays when we were small, kicking at each other for more room beneath the duvet.

"What happened?" I asked him in the dark.

"I failed end of year exams."

"But why?"

"I didn't work hard enough."

"But *why?*"

"I'm not like you. I can't just work and work and work."

"That's not all I do."

"No, I know. I mean, I can't keep at something. I just didn't care enough."

"What will you do?"

He shrugged beneath the duvet. "I'll sort it out."

*   *   *

When I was young, I knew only that there were people who had a hard time of it, and people who did not. When I grew older, and came to understand what the trouble in our family meant, I thought that there was a way to escape it. And while I learned, eventually, that neither of my beliefs were even close to the fact of it all, it still lingered in me, the fear that it was my fault because I didn't think to warn my brother. I was so hell bent on swimming away from the riptide that I never thought to look back and check his distance from the shore.

*   *   *

I won a prize in my final year of medical school. It was for an abstract I presented at a conference in Berlin. *How to Break a Heart: The Emerging Role of Epigenetics in the Pathogenesis of Cardiovascular Disease.* I swayed nervous on the lino of the conference hall while stale, old men in shirts and chinos, and frowning women in skirt suits, held their chins. Occasionally they'd ask a question, and I stumbled over my answers, despite having prepared a response to every critique I could imagine.

I had turned my phone off. It wasn't until much later, after the conference drinks, and the drinks after the drinks, that I got back to my hotel room and checked for messages. Which was when I heard my mother's strangled voice on the answerphone saying that Lewis had put himself in hospital again.

* * *

If I went back to the beach with the mussels, and our buckets, and the rain, and the peat, and if Lewis had squinted at me once more through the fog as I pulled a stringy mussel from its rock, I'd say,

"The will to survive is strong, Lewis. It's stronger than consciousness. They don't cling to the rocks because they want to live, but because they must not die."

* * *

He had a canula in the back of his hand attached to an IV drip hanging off a hook on a metal stand. There were a couple of get-well cards. I looked at them while he crunched ice.

Wishing you a speedy recovery!

"Mum and dad didn't tell them why I was here," he said, then bit down with a crack.

Outside the paper walls of the cubicle there came familiar, disjointed hospital noises. Beeps, squeaks of wheels on plastic, rustling papers, coughs, the occasional moan.

"What will you do?" I asked.

"I'm getting better," he said.

"But what does that mean?"

He rolled his eyes. "You're the doctor. You tell me."

"Are you going to stay with mum and dad?"

He sighed and looked out of the window.

"I don't know."

"I'd have you with me but..."

He put his fingers to the bridge of his nose and pinched, hard.

* * *

My mother's heart started doing strange runs.

Up and down she said. *It's like it's running up and down the inside of my chest.* I thought it was probably too much coffee, but I sent her to the GP anyway, and he sent her to a real cardiologist. They did an ECG and said it was nothing that they could see. Nothing physiological. They said it was probably too much coffee.

141

I know what my father thought. He thought it was purely of the body, only it wasn't my mother's body that was doing the damage.

* * *

He disappeared for four months, and a silence closed around our family. The thing that held my brother left no ransom notes. I went to his bedroom, searched through his things to see if I could find phone numbers, addresses.

He'd left his laptop and I read his search history: YouTube videos of his favourite bands, search questions – *how tall is the Dalai Lama? Can you get bats bigger than humans?* – and Reddit threads – *Are SSRIs worth it? My family hates me.*

He'd saved all his logins, so I scrolled through his Facebook friends. There were only a few I recognised. I wasn't sure whether to message anyone. I didn't want to embarrass him. In the end I contacted some old school friends. Only one answered, a few days later.

Haven't seen Lewis since sixth form. Have you got hold of him? Hope he's doing OK. I know he struggled, sometimes.

* * *

It was a beast that ate my brother. That's the way Mum always talked of it. It was a beast that sunk its teeth in and wouldn't let go. Every time we managed to pry the jaws of the beast open, pull it away from his bruised and battered body, we would think that we had won. But none of us – me, my mum, my dad – had the strength to hold it off indefinitely. It always slunk back towards him, and no matter how many times we yelled, no matter how we screamed and waved our arms, he wouldn't run away.

* * *

When Lewis returned, he came to me first. He knocked on my door with no warning and I stood in the doorway for a good ten seconds before I thought to bring him indoors.

"Are they pissed?" he said.

There were many things I wanted to say, but instead, I said,

"I missed you."

I let him sleep in my bed, and I stayed on the sofa. I told him it was because he needed the rest. I watched the front door mirrored in the living room window. My pale, stretched face sharpened into focus as the patio darkened to black.

By early morning, my body was seizing up from the contortions it took to stay on the narrow cushions. When Orna came home from her night shift she said,

"You look like shit."

She made me a tea, and then, while she showered, I pulled Lewis' clothes from his rucksack to wash. They stank. The fibres were clogged with filth. I did not recognise them.

Orna was in bed by the time Lewis got up. We moved around each other gently, quietly. He made cornflakes and said,

"You're watching me."

"You should eat something more substantial," I said.

"I always liked cornflakes."

"You used to put loads of sugar on them."

"Mum hated it."

"She was terrified of what the dentist would say if you needed fillings. That he would think she was a bad mother."

"I have perfect teeth, though. Even now," said Lewis. He pulled his lips back in a grimace.

"I called in sick," I said.

He put his spoon down in his bowl.

"I wish you hadn't."

"What else am I supposed to do?"

"I hate the attention."

I took the cereal box off the table, and shoved my hand inside. I pulled out a handful of flakes, put them in my mouth and chewed. They were so dry, they sucked up all my saliva.

*　*　*

In my first year as a junior doctor, I worked a rotation on A & E. I was surprised by how quickly I came to see people as bodies to be fixed. How swiftly the person sunk away, leaving only bone and muscle, flesh and blood. How soon I came to define a patient as a litany of damage. The woman with the stroke, the boy with the knife wound, the man with burns. I knew that it was impossible to do otherwise, would require you to work against an insurmountable acknowledgement of pain. Or perhaps that is what I told myself for comfort. To reassure myself that I wasn't simply afraid of what understanding the pain might do to me.

* * *

When we went to our parents, my dad explained to Lewis all the trouble he was causing, how upset he was making our mother, how he needed to *grow the fuck up now*, because he was *twenty-two and not fourteen.*

"He could just stop," he said over and over, after my mum had rushed outside to comfort Lewis, yapping at his heels like an anxious puppy. I could see them through the kitchen window, her holding his hand, stroking it aggressively, like she could force her love into him.

"It's a disease, Dad," I said. "If he could stop, he would."

"What you mean is he can't help himself."

"Exactly."

"Which sounds like a convenient excuse."

And I thought, wasn't it at least a little true.

* * *

On that same holiday in Ireland, as we clambered over the rocks, Lewis slipped and sliced his heel open. The cut was deep, and it bled a lot. I made him bathe it in a rockpool.

"The salt cleans it," I said.

"It stings," he said. He didn't cry.

"A lot?"

"I don't know," he said. "What's a lot?"

"Well, does it hurt?"

"I think so."

It turned into a little ridge of scar, an unusual shape, like a hook. The kind of mark you might use to identify a body.

* * *

When I returned from work, Orna was on the sofa. She looked up at me as I came in through the door, and I said,

"What's happened?"

"No, nothing," she said. "It's just ... he's being a bit ... odd."

Lewis was in my bedroom. He was sitting on the floor, headphones on, his phone by his thigh. He was holding the neck of a bottle of red wine.

"What are you doing?" I asked.

He did not look up. He was singing, quietly, tunelessly. I knelt down, pulled a headphone from his ear. "What are you doing, Lewis?"

He squinted one eye at my face. "Listening to music."

"You're drunk?"

"It's OK."

"On your own? Lewis, you're drunk on your own."

He waved his hand at me, as if swatting a fly. I took hold of the wine. I put my hands beneath his armpits and lifted him onto the bed. He started to giggle, and I shoved him hard.

"You're so selfish," I said. "You're so fucking selfish."

*   *   *

In my first foundation year, I met Nish. I wondered when I should tell him about the strange appendage I had, which was my brother.

"What are your family like?" he said one night, his breath in my ear, his body hot against mine beneath the covers.

"They're nice. Normal."

"Normal?"

"Mm."

"What does normal mean, when it comes to families?" He said.

"Boring, I suppose."

"My family aren't normal, then."

"Do they worry you?"

"No, they don't worry me," he said. "They annoy me. They are very *interested* in me."

I worried on nights when Nish stayed over that Lewis would appear at the door, his bag in his hand. I worried he'd turn up at my hospital and ask for me at the department reception. I worried whenever my phone rang, because the only people who phoned rather than messaged were Lewis, or my mum with news of Lewis.

"Interested how?"

He yawned. I could smell toothpaste and the anchovies on his breath from dinner. "They think my life is their business."

"That's love, isn't it?"

"Ha. Yes. Love. Overwhelming, stifling love."

*   *   *

When he disappeared again, I didn't go home. I took the phone call from my mum, and I said,

"Well, keep me updated."

I carried on working. My mum carried on going to her Spanish classes.

I messaged Lewis's number, even though it always stayed unread: *just let us know you're alright.*

I met my dad for coffee because he was in the city for work, and he rubbed his face. He had become thinner, his skin too big for his bones. It hung heavy like tent canvas around his eyes, at his chin.

"I just wish it was different, for your mum's sake," he said. The whites of his eyes were tinted pink.

"I think Mum's got used to it."

"Your mum won't ever get used to it. She's just become better at ignoring it."

I sipped at my cappuccino.

"You'd tell us, wouldn't you? If you knew anything," my dad said.

"You're really asking?"

"You've always been so close. I know you'd not want to let him down."

"I'm an adult. I know where the lines are."

"Yes, yes. Sorry, you're a good girl."

* * *

I had helped fit a patient with a pacemaker, and in the follow up consultation he said,

"I'm half robot now."

His wife was beside him. She laughed, but I could tell it was a nervous laugh. She kept patting at the edge of his dressing. When the consultation was complete, and I had closed the curtains of his bed, the wife slipped out and tapped me on the arm.

"I don't want to sound silly –" she said.

"There are no stupid questions," I said.

"But, could it break? Could it make his heart go wrong?"

"There is always a small chance of a malfunction. But it's very slim. About one in every thousand have problems. And if there's any concern, you can come straight back here."

She fiddled with the lapel of her jacket.

"I just don't like the idea of it. Of something inside him, controlling his heart. Something that's not him."

"It's better than no control," I said.

She patted her chest, where her own heart would be. "I'm scared of going to sleep," she said in a whisper. "I'm scared that I'll wake up and he'll be dead next to me."

I had pushed a key under a stone by the front door, and messaged Lewis so he'd know where to find it.

"We'll get robbed," said Nish.

"What if I'm not here, when he comes?"

"Then he'll have to wait."

"He might leave again."

"Well, you'd never know."

"That's not the point," I said.

We were getting ready for Orna's wedding. We needed to get three different trains spread over six hours to reach a small village in Cornwall.

"I'm going to put my tie on when I get there," said Nish, and he shoved it in his jacket pocket. "We can't leave a key out all weekend."

"No one is going to rob us."

"He can go to your parents."

"He wouldn't."

"Look, what are the odds he'll come anyway? Really?"

I stopped searching for my good clutch at the bottom of the wardrobe. "He's always come back."

"He's twenty-eight. He's a grown man."

"So?"

"So, isn't it time he faced his own consequences?"

I stood up, the clutch in my hand. It was the only designer thing I owned and I'd bought it years ago, on a whim, when I'd passed my final year exams. Lewis had a job then, in a call centre. He'd liked it, he said, because it was so busy you never got a chance to think. When older people rang for help with their mobile phone accounts he always went over the allotted call time.

"You're talking like he deserves all this."

"No, obviously not. I just mean – look, it's not my place to say."

"And yet?"

Nish took a deep breath. "I just feel – he doesn't have to leave you in limbo all the time. It's selfish."

"He's not selfish," I said. Lewis came into my mind, as a ten-year-old standing on a damp Irish beach. His bucket empty because he could not bear to cause pain to a mollusc. "He's never been selfish."

"Ok," Nish held his hands up.

"Just because you hate your family."

Nish opened his mouth to say something, then closed it again. He picked up his rucksack. "We need to go. The train."

I made sure the key was well hidden before we left.

*   *   *

I passed my final cardiology exam, got my sign offs, and started applying for consultant positions. By then, Lewis had been back, then gone, then come back again. Occasionally he stayed with me and Nish, mostly with my parents. He'd taken to leaving notes, always something like,

Taking a bit of a break, be back soon

Needed to clear my head

Sometimes he'd come back at the end of the day, other times it'd be weeks. Once, it was months. My dad kept every note he left, tucked them in his desk drawer in the study.

*   *   *

When I got my first consultant post, I took everyone out for dinner to a fancy restaurant. Our mum drank too much wine. She put her napkin to her eyes, and then held a glass over the remnants of her desert and said,

"I'm so proud," and she pointed her glass at me, then at Lewis. "Of you both. Of you both."

Lewis looked at his lap. Nish slid his hand in mine.

On the walk back to the tube Lewis came up to my side. He had his hands deep in his pockets.

"Is this all because of me?" he said.

"Dinner?"

"No, not dinner. I mean, you being this great doctor. Doing so well."

"I'm not a great doctor, I'm just a normal doctor. And no. What's that got to do with you?"

He shrugged. "I thought, maybe, you felt you had to be extra good. To make up for me."

I looked out at the Thames, the reflected lights rolling in the waves.

"You sound like you've been having therapy," I said.

"I have."

"That's good. I wanted to be a psychiatrist, once."

"But you didn't become one."

"No."

"Why not?"

I pulled my coat more tightly around my middle. "Want to go to the theatre in a couple of weeks? The hospital does this thing with tickets. Discounts for staff. We could go and see something?"

"Yeah, alright," he said.

"In a couple of weeks?"

"Yes."

"OK," I said. "But don't worry, if something else comes up. We can go another time."

"Sure," he said. "But I'll come."

We left Lewis and my parents at the Victoria line, and took the Northern. I rested my head on Nish's shoulder and watched our faces flicker clear then blurry in the carriage window. Back at the flat, Nish let himself in. I crouched by the front step, and turned over a stone. I picked up the key – damp and cold and rusted on one edge by time – and slipped it into my pocket.

MIKE KILGANNON

Enough

" *I hope you've brought enough for everyone"* says Sister Triona, even though she knows I haven't, and she knows I've only the one glued to the roof of my mouth, and she knows it's only a lemon sherbet, not what you could call a mortal sin, and she knows I'm not one to break a rule and suck a sweet in class and she knows I know better and she knows what she's at the auld bitch making every head turn my way and how the blood will run to my cheeks and how if I'd a thousand lemon sherbets I'd hand them round and round and round if it got their eyes off me and back to the sums on the blackboard and she knows I'm from good stock not allowed sweets in Lent so she knows I didn't bring it from home and she knows where I got it from and she knows where I get them every Tuesday after swimming and after prayers and before sums and she knows and she knows and she knows

JAIME GILL

Eulogy of Henry Rowley, 1961-2024 (Notes)

~~Quote Tennyson's "In Memoriam"? No. Beautiful but stodgy. Also, not sure it IS better to have loved and lost.~~

Auden's "Funeral Blues? ~~Cliched, though Henry didn't notice cliches.~~ "He was my North, South, East, West." YES. Henry: my world.

Our first date: Greenwich planetarium. A tinny, recorded voice described earth and moon locked together. ~~But not forever.~~

Henry: Earth. Expansive, beautiful, explosively alive.

Me: Moon. Complete with dark side. ~~Often eclipsed.~~

Afterwards, Henry took me to my first gay bar. Frightened but excited. Everyone stared at him. Some glanced my way, wondering why he'd picked me. I didn't know either. *Note: make funny, not pathetic.*

Our whole life together like that. His personality so big its gravity pulled people in. ~~I attracted people only because I was in his orbit.~~ His acting career bloomed like rainforests. Mine waxed and waned... mostly waned. *Remember: make it funny.*

He was generous with his light and life – ~~his sympathy felt like pity.~~ ~~So cold in his great shadow.~~

Fact: real moon is slowly leaving earth at same speed fingernails grow. ~~Slow separation's more painful than sudden. Love cools with every millimetre of distance. Resentment creeps in the gaps.~~

Fact: moon and earth were born from same gas cloud. ~~Will also die together, incinerated as dying sun swells.~~

~~But I'm not dead.~~

He's gone, and all life with him.

~~Now I'm free. Could create life of my own. Want to, but it's so late. I'm old. That dying sun's reaching for me too.~~

KAREN WHITELAW

Love Bite

The chef's husband comes home late with someone else's love bite under his collar. She sees it when they're undressing for bed. She hunkers down in the shower, under scalding water, and stares at the tiles where the grout is coming loose. When the pain of her burning skin is worse than the pain inside, she turns off the tap. Lathers soap into every centimetre of skin, every cranny, hides under the white foam. Then on with the cold water, shocking the suds away from her body, down her legs and she's naked again. Boiled red. Exposed.

Her husband is already asleep, or feigning sleep, she can't tell which. She stands over him, stares at the long nose she once thought patrician, at his wispy grey hairline, his deceitful neck. With both hands she traces her breastbone like she's measuring for CPR. But it's the soft tissue underneath the sternum she wants. She forces her fingers into it and digs deep, so deep her skin splits. Her fingertips claw in, peeling skin off flesh. Her ribs are harder to crack but her chef's hands are strong from years of breaking carcasses of chicken, pork, veal. She opens herself up. Tears into the connecting tissue and muscles and wrenches out her heart. Places it on the floor next to him. Then she rolls up beside it, her toes in her mouth like a haddock arranged on a plate, dishing herself up to him.

SALLY CURTIS

Jenny's Mum Tells Lies

Jenny's mum says Jenny can't play today because she's feeling poorly and has to stay in but, through the window round the back, Jenny tells me she's not sick but her mum doesn't want to tell me the truth and I ask her what the truth is, but Jenny says her mum won't tell her either but she knows it's something to do with my mum so, when I get home, I ask mum what the something is that means Jenny's mum won't let Jenny play with me and Mum says Jenny's mum is a gossiping b-word and should mind her own f-word-ing business and I ought to make other friends even though I try to explain how Jenny is my very best friend and I'll miss her, but Mum says I'll get over it because kids my age make new friends all the time and, besides, Jenny's mum is a stuck-up cow who's always boasting about her colour TV and shag-pile carpet and Jenny will grow up to be the same, mark her words, and won't want anything to do with me in the end like all the others who live in the houses near the park with the big lawns and, clipping on her sparkliest earrings and checking herself in the mirror, she puckers her bright red lips and reminds me our sort knows what's what.

Before she leaves, she chucks my chin and then dabs her wrists with the perfume Jenny's dad gave her last week.

EMMA LEVIN

Flat Five

Not long after you moved, into the very top of an old, looming apartment block, you met her. Your neighbour. A pleasant girl, agreeable. She occupied each of the other four flats in the building: always entering and exiting, from one door, from another.

Did she think she was fooling you with the costumes she wore? Of course, anyone could tell she was only one person masquerading around as four, each with a different laugh, name, accent, gait. You had never seen anything like it.

But months passed, and you said nothing. After all, how delightful it was to hear her silky piano from flat three, or smell her pancakes cooking from flat one. Some mornings she'd even deliver you a plate.

Recently, you had seen her wearing the same style of jacket you wore to work. You laughed a little, noting the colour was a shade off. It was a mistake she never repeated.

And when she knocked on your door, one bright autumn day, to ask if you'd seen her keys (for the fifth flat, where she lived), you smiled and handed them over. She thanked you graciously, smiling that very same smile, and walked inside. You watched as she took off her jacket and hung it up.

Such a polite girl. Explaining, with faint mirth, that she had to take an important call. No, no, you didn't want to intrude. You apologised, chuckling, and opened the window.

Your body released. It certainly was a long way down.

MAIRGHREAD McLUNDIE

My Aunt Keeps a Spider in Her Hairnet

The result, she confessed, of a bathtime rescue gone awry: a speck of flotsam draggled over a sheet of toilet paper hastily procured to absorb excess moisture; her conscience prepared for the burden of yet another small life.

But by morning it had moved; her eight-legged Lazarus lurked in the grout, a disconsolate smudge between the hostile sheen of tiles. He surveyed and scurried across and down, but after three days there was still no web.

My aunt (anxious to be hospitable) placed a net sponge at his disposal; he seemed not to mind its violent hue, and it attracted flies if left unrinsed from cleaning tidemarks off the bath. But they buzzed away before Arthur (as she'd taken to calling him) could pounce. Too much bounce, she concluded. And not enough stick.

Concerned his exoskeleton seemed duller, she retrieved a near-dead fly from the windowsill and placed it near her guest. Then watched, with a relish that alarmed her, as the prey was digested and the husk left, lifeless.

But, she conceded, that could not persist. She dismissed fly-paper: too indiscriminate. How is it, she considered, that spiders do not stick to their own orb? She consulted the Web: only the spiral threads adhere. Hard to imitate; she feared she'd need to weave a different trap.

At the chemist's, she chose a hairnet of close and very fine filament. Now, of an evening, they sit: window ajar, the standard lamp a Siren sun, reading Kafka and waiting.

ADAM Z. ROBINSON

The story we will one day never tire of telling you

You washed up overnight, attended by gossiping crabs, in your rock pool nursery. Your skin smelled of seaweed and sulphur. You blew ocean foam bubbles; your snot tasted like oyster. Your head was worn smooth like a pebble, your fontanel scallop-soft under our adoring, wondering thumbs.

We swaddled you in plastic netting and marine litter, made you a bonnet from a skate's egg case, gave you a cuttlefish bone to cut your teeth.

When we weaned you it was on candy floss and rock, whizzed with Mr Whippy. As soon as you were old enough for solids, we bought hot, fresh doughnuts and wadded them into balls. You opened your mouth like a Skee-Ball clown; we *ooh*ed and *aah*ed.

In your nappy we'd find garishly-coloured eggs that held prizes of plastic racing cars, joke spiders and rose-shaped rings that squirted water.

You laughed like a policeman trapped in a glass box and cried the mechanical melody of *Oh My Darling Clementine*. We bathed you on the log flume, burped you on the carousel. The g-force of the waltzers provoked a growth spurt.

Before you arrived, we'd tried everything. Somebody told us that the seaside was good for people in our situation. Something about the sea air, the relaxation, the fun. Nonsense. But we would have done anything, anything.

When our arms started to ache under you, we found a balloon stall, filled you up with helium. We walked the pier proudly, holding onto your string until our knuckles turned white.

ALISON WASSELL

Chicken

"She won't do it," Lauren says, pointing at you. "She's chicken. Crying already." The others have already stuck their hands into the box where the dead thing is, withdrawn sick-faced. You've never talked to Lauren before, don't know the names of the other girls, are only here, in your neighbour's shed, because Gran needed somewhere to leave you, and Lauren's mum offered, because this morning you can't be in the house, not with all that's going on, all that needs to be done. You're not chicken, and you tell her so.

"Dare you, then," she says. You rub your swollen eyes with your fists, roll up your sleeve and thrust your hand through the clumsy hole she's made in the cardboard box. Your fingers touch flesh, but you don't flinch. You know what a raw chicken breast feels like. You rip off the lid and, smirking, show the others.

"Kids' stuff," you say.

You're lion-brave, not chicken-scared. You think of things you've touched that prove it. A slug, dog poop, your grandfather's fish-bait maggots, a half-eaten rat, brought home by the cat, the pheasant Uncle Simon shot, lying plucked and ripped open on the kitchen table, your best friend's warm vomit, that time she was sick over your desk at school, handfuls of hair clogging the bathroom sink, blood stained phlegm on a cotton pillow, the cracked, chapped lips of your ten-minutes-dead mum as you kissed her, just now, before you left the house.

Biographies

Judges' Biographies

Liz Berry is an award-winning poet and author of the critically acclaimed collections *Black Country* (Chatto, 2014); *The Republic of Motherhood* (Chatto, 2018); *The Dereliction* (Hercules Editions, 2021) and *The Home Child* (Chatto, 2023), a novel in verse. Liz's work, described as "a sooty soaring hymn to her native West Midlands" (*Guardian*), celebrates the landscape, history and dialect of the region. Liz has received the Somerset Maugham Award, Geoffrey Faber Memorial Prize and Forward Prizes. Her poem 'Homing', a love poem for the language of the Black Country, is part of the GCSE English syllabus.

Wendy Erskine's two short story collections *Sweet Home* and *Dance Move* are published by The Stinging Fly Press and Picador. For Paper Visual Art Books she edited *well I just kind of like it*, an anthology of writing on art in the home and the home as art. Her writing on art, music and books has appeared widely and she is a regular interviewer and broadcaster. She hosts a radio show on Soho Radio for Rough Trade Books. In 2021 she was Seamus Heaney Fellow at Queen's University Belfast and in 2023 she became a Fellow of the Royal Society of Literature. She is a full-time secondary school teacher.

Jasmine Sawers is a Kundiman fellow and Indiana University MFA alum. Their work has won awards from *Ploughshares*, *NANO Fiction*, *Fractured Lit*, and Press 53, and has appeared in such journals and anthologies as Norton's *Flash Fiction America*, *Best Microfiction*, *SmokeLong Quarterly*, and *Wigleaf*. Their book, *The Anchored World*, was a finalist for the 2023 PEN/Robert W. Bingham Prize for Debut Short Story Collection. Originally from Buffalo, Sawers now lives outside St. Louis.

Writers' Biographies

Houssam Alissa is the son of immigrants, born in London to an Iraqi GP and an Indian college lecturer. From a young age, they read him the greats (Chicken Licken, Puddle Lane, etc); fostering in him an early love of reading. Despite their entirely sensible pleas for him to consider medicine, he went on to study English at the University of Nottingham. He spent a few years teaching English in Russia before returning to the UK where he succeeded in selling his soul to a corporation in whose servitude he remains today. He lives in Edinburgh, and occasionally writes things.

Chrissy Banks is a one-time counsellor and trainer. She lives in Exeter, runs poetry reading groups and co-hosts Uncut Poets monthly live and online. Her second collection is *The Uninvited* (Indigo Dreams 2019) and a pamphlet *Frank* (Smith Doorstop 2021) from the Poetry Business. Competition commendations include the Teignmouth and Winchester Poetry Competitions 2021. She was shortlisted for the Bridport Prize 2021 and Teignmouth's Devon Poets prize, 2023 and long listed for the Live Canon Open and Waltham Forest Competitions in 2022. Poems also in many journals and anthologies. Recent reviews in the High Window.

Joe Bedford is an author from Doncaster, UK. His short stories have been published widely, including in *3:AM*, *Evening Standard, Litro* and elsewhere. His stories have also won numerous awards including the Leicester Writes Prize, as well as being longlisted for the Commonwealth Short Story Prize, the Fish Short Story Prize and the ALCS Tom-Gallon Award among others. Since 2021 he has curated *Writers on Research* – an ongoing craft interview series exploring the research methods of over fifty contemporary authors. His debut novel *A Bad Decade for Good People* was published by Parthian Books in Summer 2023.

CJ Bowman is a doctor who lives and works in London. He also holds a Masters-of-Arts in Creative Writing. *Thump Thump* is his first short story to be published. Find him on Instagram @conor.bowman

Sally Curtis lives close to the sea and is a burnt-out teacher, happy hypnotherapist, and would-be novelist. She has a number of micros, flash fictions and short stories published online and in paper form and has been successful in many competitions including winning the Retreat West Microfiction prize and Flash Fiction prize, Writing Magazine's 500 word, and placed with Flash 500. Recently, one of her stories was featured on BBC

Uploads. Sally presented a Flash Fiction workshop at the Bournemouth Writing Festival last year and hopes to do so again this year. At present, she is writing a Novella-in-Flash. https://www.facebook.com/sallywritesstories

Francesca Duffield is a writer and artist from the English Midlands now living in Lewes, East Sussex. She has poems published in the London Independent Story Prize 'Rising Stars' Anthology 2023, the 2023 and 2024 anthologies by Artemisia Arts and Mosaique Press, three anthologies of the 'Bourne to Write' writers group, and 'Ingenue Magazine'. She participated in a European translations project with the poet John Eliot and Mosaique Press, and her poem translated into Romanian will be included in the book 'Cross-Currents 2'. She has worked as an illustrator and art lecturer, and when not writing, creates paintings and prints.

Rosalind Easton is a poet and teacher from South East London. After a first degree in English, she trained as a dancer and spent several years teaching ballet, modern and tap before returning to university for her PGCE and MA. Her debut pamphlet *Black Mascara (Waterproof)* was a winner in the Poetry Business International Book & Pamphlet Competition in 2020, and her second *Man Overboard* won the Paper Swans Press Pamphlet Prize in 2022. She received her PhD in English Literature from Birkbeck College, University of London in 2021. Find her on Instagram – Rosalind_Easton_poet and X – @Rosalind_Easton

T.N. Eyer is an ex-lawyer who has happily transitioned to writing fiction full time. Her first novel, *Finding Meaning in the Age of Immortality*, was published by Stillhouse Press in 2023. Her short fiction has appeared in a handful of literary magazines and anthologies, and her story "Date of Death" was listed as a Distinguished Story in *Best American Short Stories 2022*. In addition to writing, she enjoys hiking, traveling, and playing Dance Dance Revolution. She lives in Pittsburgh with her husband and daughter. Find her on Instagram @ tneyerwriter and www.tneyer.com

Jaime Gill is a British-born writer living in Cambodia. His stories have appeared in *Litro*, *The Phare*, *Fiction Attic*, *Good Life Review*, *Scribes*, and more. He won the 2024 Honeybee Literature Prize for Short Story, Berlin Literary Review's 2024 Best Flash Fiction award, and is a nominee for Best of The Net 2024. He's also won or been a finalist for awards including New Writers 2024, the Bridport Prize, Flash405, Masters Review, and the Bath Short Story Award. He's currently working on a novel, script, and far, far too many stories. More at www.jaimegill.com.

Roshni Goyate is a poet, a mother, a proud daughter of Indian immigrants and founder of Tenderly, where she runs writing workshops for people to come back to their creative selves. She's part of the 4 BROWN GIRLS WHO WRITE collective, and has published a pamphlet called *Shadow Work*, in the *4 BROWN GIRLS WHO WRITE* pamphlet collection (Rough Trade Books 2020). Her work has also been included in *Poetry Unbound: 50 Poems to Open Your World*, edited by Padraig O'Tuama (Canongate 2022). Roshni hails from north-west London and spends her time between Muscat and London. @roshnigoyate @tenderly.xyz @4browngirlswhowrite

Linnhe Harrison was born in Chester in 1977 and spent her home-ed childhood between North Wales and the Lake District. She now lives in Kirkby Stephen, Cumbria with her musician husband and two children. Entirely self-taught, Linnhe worked as an animator and as a sailing instructor prior to moving into graphic design and marketing. Having previously dabbled in shorter forms of creative writing, she started working on what would become her debut novel in the summer of 2023. Dark, speculative and dystopian, *The Incredible Machines of Thinkery: Outpost 9* was self-published in July 2024.

Kenneth Havey was born in London and began writing at the age of 55, an old dog stirred to new tricks by the cumulative inspiration of years of reading well. He describes his experience of writing as a daily oscillation between promise and deflation, and as a welcome, if consistently unappeasable, compulsion. The author of numerous short stories, Kenneth is currently writing two novels which draw, thematically, on his past experiences of mental illness; he always works on at least two stories at the same time. Kenneth lives with his stoical wife and their arthritic terrier in the foothills of Crete's Dikti Mountains.

Luisa A. Igloria is the author of *Caulbearer* (Immigrant Writing Series Prize, Black Lawrence Press, 2024), *Maps for Migrants and Ghosts* (Co-Winner, 2019 Crab Orchard Open Poetry Prize), 12 other books, and 4 chapbooks. She is lead editor, with co-editors Aileen Cassinetto and Jeremy S. Hoffman, of *Dear Human at the Edge of Time: Poems on Climate Change in the U.S.* (Paloma Press, 2023). Originally from Baguio City, she makes her home in Norfolk VA where she is the Louis I. Jaffe and University Professor of English and Creative Writing at Old Dominion University's MFA Creative Writing Program. Luisa is the 20th Poet Laureate of the Commonwealth of Virginia (2020-22), Emerita.

During her term, the Academy of American Poets awarded her a 2021 Poet Laureate Fellowship. www.luisaigloria.com

Joanne Key lives in Cheshire. Completely in love with poetry and short stories, she writes every day. Her poetry has been published in various places and won a number of prizes, including: second prize in the National Poetry Competition, 2014; first prize in the Hippocrates Open Prize, 2018; first prize in Buzzwords Prize, 2020 and first prize in the Working Class Nature Writing Prize, 2021. Her work has been shortlisted in several competitions, including The Bridport Prize, and has also been highly commended or commended in others. She is also a past winner of the Mslexia Short Story Competition.

Mike Kilgannon is an English teacher and dad living in Sheffield. He grew up in St Helens, Merseyside and has been scribbling in secret ever since. His flash fiction piece *The Hercules Reopened* won second place in the Bridport Prize in 2019. Another flash fiction piece, *To Dust*, won third place in the 2022 New Writers competition.

Melissa Knox Evans grew up in Rome and currently lives in Oxford, UK. Her poetry has recently appeared or is forthcoming in *New York Quarterly, Barzakh Magazine, Stoneboat Literary Journal, Broad River Review*, and elsewhere. She received a Pushcart nomination in 2023, placed third in the Plaza Prize in Poetry (2024) and was a finalist in the Rash Award in Poetry (2024). Evans is creative director of science and arts publication, *Seisma Magazine*.

Clare Labrador is a writer from the Philippines. She has a Bachelor's Degree in Creative Writing from the Ateneo de Manila University. Her work has appeared in Gulf Coast, Booth, and Waxwing.

Andrew Laurence has been a barrister, puppeteer, actor, and head of a top London PR agency. He studied at the Inns of Court School of Law, the Webber Douglas Academy of Dramatic Art and has an MA in Creative Writing from Goldsmiths. In addition to short stories he has written five novels, two of which are self-published, and one acquired by a leading publisher in Italy. He is currently finishing a novel set in 1973 about a small-town Logan Roy bent on making millions when government policy triggers a housebuilding boom. Andrew lives in South London.

Emma Levin is an 18 year old writer living in London, starting her first year of university studying English Literature, having previously studied Fine Art and Politics. She greatly enjoys creating intricate narratives and characters, through both short stories and short plays. Inspired by gothic and modernist authors, her aim is to balance surrealism and the ordinary within her writing. She also adores life drawing and digital art, with writing and art forming two sides of the coin of her spare time.

Shanna McGoldrick is a journalist who grew up in Lancashire and now lives in Manchester. She recently started writing poems, inconsistently, while her young son naps or when the rest of the house is asleep. The advantage of this approach is that tiredness occasionally brings with it a strange kind of creative clarity. The disadvantage is that her house is a mess and she is permanently behind on everything. She was the winner of the 2023 Passionfruit Poetry Prize.

Tom McLaughlin is a Derry-born poet who grew up on both sides of the Irish border. His debut pamphlet, *Open Houses*, was published in 2021 with Marble Press. He completed an MA in Creative Writing, with Distinction, at Royal Holloway and is a practice-based PhD candidate at Surrey University. His poems have recently featured in anthologies by Arachne Press and Broken Sleep, and he won first prize in Cannon's Mouth 2024 Sonnet or Not Competition. You can find out more at https://tommclaughlin.uk/

Mairghread McLundie has a background in computing science and design/craft. In 2006 she completed a Ph.D. examining aspects of creative processes and was an academic researcher at Glasgow School of Art's Digital Design Studio until 2008. In 2009 she began attending courses in creative writing (poetry and fiction) at the University of Glasgow's Centre for Open Studies. Her work has been published in various anthologies, and in 2019 she was shortlisted for the Wigtown Poetry Prize and longlisted in the National Poetry Competition. She lives near Glasgow in an old stone house with her husband and many, many spiders.

Kat Nugent is a writer and editorial consultant living in north London. She grew up between Jakarta, Indonesia and Perth, Australia before moving to Scotland to study English Literature and History at the University of Edinburgh. She completed an MA in Creative Writing at Goldsmiths University and in 2023, her work was longlisted for the Pat Kavanagh Prize. She is currently working on her first novel.

Emily Rinkema lives and writes in northern Vermont, USA. Her writing has recently appeared in *The Sun Magazine*, *SmokeLong Quarterly*, and *X-R-A-Y Lit*, and she has stories in the *Best American Nonrequired Reading*, Bath Flash and Oxford Flash anthologies. You can read her work on her website https://emilyrinkema.wixsite.com/my-site or follow her on X or IG (@emilyrinkema).

Adam Z. Robinson is a theatre writer, performer and author of flash fiction. His original theatre credits include: *Unhomely* (2024), *Belle and Mary* (2021), *Upon the Stair* (2020), *Smile Club* (co-written with Andrea Heaton, 2020) and *Shivers* (2018). In flash fiction, in 2023 his story 'Favouritism' won joint first place in The Letter Review's flash fiction competition, his story 'Assembly Line' was published in the Bath Flash Fiction Anthology and his story 'God Save the King' was highly commended in the Bridport Prize. Adam is the host of The Ghost Story Book Club podcast. Find him on X @adam_zed and Instagram @adam__zed (two underscores on Instagram)

Anna Round grew up in Belfast and Glasgow and studied English at Oxford University before moving to London. She now lives in Newcastle-upon-Tyne in the North East of England, where she works in research. Her short stories have appeared in the *Fish* anthology, the 2023 *Best Mystery Stories of the Year* collection, the Hammond House anthology and elsewhere. She is a former winner of the Briar Cliff and Sid Chaplin short story awards and is currently working on a novel. When not writing she enjoys running very long distances, snowboarding, and music (especially Beethoven and Bruce Springsteen).

Charlotte Salkind is a writer and documentary filmmaker and lives in London. She is one of the Genesis Foundation's ten Emerging Writers for 2024-25 and is working on her first collection. She has been shortlisted previously for the Bridport Prize and was a finalist in the Troubadour International Poetry Prize. She has directed and produced on documentary series for National Geographic, Netflix and ITV, and her research for documentaries has been nominated for an Emmy Award.

John Tait is a Canadian-American writer whose stories have appeared in *Narrative*, *Crazyhorse*, *Prairie Schooner*, *Southwest Review*, and *The Sun* and have won prizes such as the Tobias Wolff Award, the Rick Demarinis Fiction Award, and the H.E. Francis Award for Fiction. He is an Associate Professor of Fiction at the University of North Texas.

Amy Ward's poetry has been four-times nominated for a Pushcart Prize and has appeared in *Poetry London*, *Magma*, *Spelt*, *VerseVille*, *Mslexia*, *The Frogmore Papers*, *Agenda*, *Penumbra*, among others. She's been commended in the National Poetry Competition, Mslexia's Pamphlet and Poetry competitions, the Indigo Poetry Competition, The Frogmore, Troubadour and Café Writers. Ward took part in the Places of Poetry Project for England and Wales; in partnership with the Ordnance Survey, The Poetry Society and National Poetry Day. She's a finalist for the Aesthetica Writing Award and a selection of her poetry has been showcased in the Aeolian Harp Series.

Alison Wassell is a writer of short and very short fiction from St. Helens, Merseyside, UK. Her work has been published by Fictive Dream, National Flash Fiction Day, FlashFlood Journal, The Disappointed Housewife, Gooseberry Pie, Books Ireland and elsewhere. She has twice been shortlisted for the Bath Flash Fiction Award. She was part of the judging team for the 2024 National Flash Fiction Day Micro Competition. She has no plans whatsoever to write a novel and wishes people would take flash fiction more seriously. Find her on Twitter/X and Instagram/Threads @lilysslave

Annabel White is a short story writer based in London. Her work was shortlisted for the Letter Review Prize 2023 and has been published in *Mslexia*, *Popshot* and *Litro*. She is a member of the London Library's Emerging Writers Programme 2024 where she is working on a short story collection exploring the grossness of girlhood, covering themes such as sex, pressure, body image and the internet.

Karen Whitelaw's short stories have been published internationally in literary journals and anthologies, including *Overland*, *Mascara*, *Meniscus*, *F(r)iction*, *Award Winning Australian Writing*, *Bath Flash Fiction 2023*, *Oxford Flash Fiction 2023* and *NFFD Anthology 2024*. Her prize-winning flash fiction has been adapted for short film, animation and a variety of multi-media platforms. She writes, lives and gains inspiration in and beside the ocean in Newcastle, Australia.

Catherine Wilson Garry is a poet and writer. Her debut poetry pamphlet *Another Word for Home is Blackbird* was published in 2023 by Stewed Rhubarb Press. Her writing has been commissioned by BBC Radio 4 and the British National Gallery. She is the winner of the Janet Coats Memorial Prize and highly commended by the Edwin Morgan Poetry

Award 2024. In 2023, she was selected as one of The London Library's Emerging Writers. She is also part of the team behind Push the Boat Out Festival, Edinburgh's International Poetry Festival, where she runs their monthly night Rock the Boat.

Angela Wipperman lives in London. She has published short fiction in *Litro, The Forge*, and elsewhere. She placed third in the 2021 Bridport prize for Flash Fiction and was shortlisted for the Retreat West first chapters prize. She is writing her first novel.